# A NEW UNIVERSAL DREAM

**My Journey from Silicon Valley
to a Life in Service to Humanity**

# A NEW UNIVERSAL DREAM

## My Journey from Silicon Valley to a Life in Service to Humanity

## STEVE FARRELL

Cofounder of Humanity's Team

The #1 Non-Profit Transformational Education Company in the World

Books may be purchased through booksellers or by contacting Sacred Stories Publishing.

A New Universal Dream
My Journey from Silicon Valley to a Life in Service to Humanity

Steve Farrell

Print ISBN: 978-1-958921-25-8
EBook ISBN: 978-1-958921-26-5

Library of Congress Control Number: 2023934901

Published by Light on Light Press
An imprint of Sacred Stories Publishing, Fort Lauderdale, FL

Printed in the United States of America

generations. This book will inspire your spirit as you comprehend the enormous potential of applying this information in your life.

—Bruce H. Lipton, PhD, *New York Times* bestselling author of
*The Biology of Belief*

While so many of us yearn to contribute to the world in a truly meaningful way, we often defer to our fear of giving up security for the unknown. Steve Farrell's odyssey from hometown boy to Silicon Valley wunderkind is epic in itself, but the fact that he gave up that life of wealth and status to devote himself to the upliftment of humanity should be an inspiration to us all. I know it is to me.

—Debra Poneman, world-renowned success coach

What does it mean to dream a new dream? In this courageous book, Steve Farrell takes us through his journey of hardship and awakening to the potential of a new collective future—one that he has dedicated himself to. *A New Universal Dream* is an inspiring and authentic book that may further awaken the call of sacred activism in all of us.

—Shamini Jain, PhD, author of *Healing Ourselves:*
*Biofield Science and the Future of Health*

Steve Farrell's life is a story of awakening we are all challenged to endure: from I to we, from the many to the one, and so from accumulating to serving. In sharing the truth of his journey, he details the portals of consciousness we all face, through which we can find each other, through which we might build a better world.

—Mark Nepo, author of *Surviving Storms* and *The Book of Awakening*

A fascinating, affirming, and uplifting story of a man who walks the talk when it comes to living up to the Divine Truth of Oneness. Steve Farrell is an inspiration, as is this book. Read it and feel the soul's call to remember who you are and how to make a difference in our world.

—Suzanne Giesemann, author of *Messages of Hope*

*A New Universal Dream* offers an intimate glimpse into what it takes to answer the quiet call deep within that whispers to us to follow the dictates of the heart. His journey from outward success to the challenges of a life of greater fulfillment and meaning will be an inspiration to every reader.

—Rev. Deborah Moldow, Founder of Garden of Light,
and Director of the Evolutionary Leaders Circle

Full of wisdom from varied sources and traditions that help guide us in an understanding of the need for a positive global vision for humanity, *A New Universal Dream* is a wonderful guidebook for us all. Steve is a man who walks his talk and embodies a higher level of consciousness, dedicated to positively changing the future of humanity.

—Jonathan Goldman, author of *The 7 Secrets of Sound Healing*

*A New Universal Dream* is a moving, inspiring, open, and authentic story of great courage and trust. Rather than a journey to a known destination, it tells of an ongoing vision, quest, and commitment to align with the Divine and the Oneness of which we are all a part, whether as yet, we know this or not.

—Jude Currivan, PhD, author of
*The Cosmic Hologram* and *The Story of Gaia*

This book will offer anyone who reads it a vivid smorgasbord of truths and a solid foundation for realistic hope for the future. I recommend it and respect its comprehensiveness and, most of all, celebrate the undying optimistic spirit that makes it valuable for all of us who are struggling to birth the new story of Oneness out of the death of the old one of separation.

—Andrew Harvey, author of *The Hope* and *Radical Regeneration*

I found myself inspired over and over again by the bold, caring, and clear choices Steve made to live the collective Universal Dream. The book made me smile, and it inspired me to want to go out and do more direct service work, feel more compassion for those who suffer from financial poverty, and to step more into my own mission.

—Diane Williams, Founder and President of the
Source of Synergy Foundation

*A New Universal Dream* should be read by every high school or university graduate, or anyone who wonders what next to do in life. When we die, we take nothing with us. What we leave behind is what counts, and Steve's work and the story of how he found his real calling should inspire millions to find their real calling, too.

—Ichak Adizes, PhD, Founder of the Adizes Institute

# TABLE OF CONTENTS

**Part 3—In Service to Humanity**

**Part 4—A Look Ahead**

# FOREWORD
## by Neale Donald Walsch

Is your life moving in the direction you really want to go? Does what you are doing in your daily life speak to your soul, open your heart, and expand your mind in a way that feels perfect for you?

Here's another question to contemplate for a moment: Why would a man who worked hard to make his way to the top of the Silicon Valley technology ladder suddenly abandon everything he was doing and completely change the direction of his life? And what kind of change did he make that brought him what his soul truly craved?

Did he discover some kind of magic formula others around the world are still searching for?

I think he did, and I also think his story could unlock a mystery for many people, opening a door to the kind of purposeful and fulfilling existence that make up many people's highest dream about what a profoundly wonderful life could look and feel like.

We've all heard of stories of people who have gone "from rags to riches." This is the story of someone who has gone from rags to riches to true riches—having nothing to do with money or the other trappings of so-called "worldly success." Could the path he has taken lead you to a path you can take to reach a similar dream of your own? Could this be your "escape hatch" to a life that might be more fulfilling?

There is much to be learned from this story, and once you've read it, I'm sure you'll agree.

Oh, and if you think you came upon this book by chance…think again.

# PART 1

## An Auspicious Beginning

# 1
# THE JOURNEY BEGINS

"**L**ive a life of integrity and continue to pursue your dreams, whatever those might be." Those were the words my dad said to me on June 24, 1979, over lunch together in an airport terminal before I boarded a flight from Virginia to San Francisco.

While we ate and watched the planes take off through the tall airport windows, he wanted to share his parting thoughts on the transition ahead of me. As I stood up to board the plane, his final words to me were, "See you at the top."

It felt like an auspicious moment, but little did I know at the time that years later, the very definition of the word "top" would completely change for me.

I was twenty-two, right out of college, and flying west to start my new job on the other side of the country. For the previous thirteen years, since I was nine and in the fourth grade, I had lived in northern Virginia, just outside Washington DC, and I had no idea how different the West Coast could be.

Growing up in Virginia had been a bit of a roller-coaster ride. My parents divorced in 1968 when I was eleven years old, and when my father moved out, even though he was not far away, he left my mother to raise me and my six brothers and sisters on her own. That was eight people—with seven of us ranging in age from between three and fifteen at the time—sharing the modest five-bedroom, three-bath, 1,388 square-foot home she got to keep in the divorce settlement as long as she kept up the mortgage payments.

Even though my mom came from a distinguished family, she received no money from them and worked full-time as a legal secretary to pay the bills. Her job didn't remotely tap into all her capabilities, but she had eight mouths to feed and it was the best she could do at the time, so she did it without complaint.

Unfortunately, her weekly salary wasn't enough on its own for us to make ends meet, so my six siblings and I all took jobs at an early age to cover our personal expenses. If we wanted the newest fashion, or décor for our bedroom, or simply to go on outings with friends, we needed to work for it. I landed my first job delivering newspapers in the fourth grade, even before the divorce, and continued to work part- or full-time from then on, regardless of how full my school schedule was. I went from newspapers to a string of different jobs—gas station attendant, drugstore clerk, telephone solicitor, UPS irregular-package clerk, horseback guide, grocery store clerk, and janitor.

When I needed braces in the sixth grade, my mother found an orthodontist who was willing to accept an installment plan of $10/month. So, at age eleven, I took care of that bill every month until I was able to pay it off with income I'd earned from my paper route and other jobs.

I knew how different my life was from that of my peers at the time, but I also knew I was gaining valuable work experience and responsibility at a much earlier age than they were. *Endurance* and *focus* became my friends as I demanded more of myself, which has, without question, helped me grow into the person I've become.

In 1970, I turned thirteen. The world around me was undergoing radical changes with the attitudes and behavior that had sparked in the late 1960s. In the neighborhood where we lived, many parents were divorced and there were more permissive attitudes about marijuana and other recreational drugs. Both teens and adults seemed more casual about sex.

Just after I turned fifteen, my father sat me down and asked me if I'd ever smoked pot. I hadn't yet, and I told him I didn't intend to. Quite unexpectedly, he suggested I should try it, so I did. I never became a "pot head" or anything close, but I enjoyed smoking at social functions on weekends or when my friends and I went to nearby music festivals.

I held the position of Treasurer at my high school throughout this time, and my reputation at school mattered a great deal to me, so I never went overboard with drugs or drinking. However, my parents didn't give much supervision or "parenting" to my siblings and me, so I began freely experimenting with both drugs and sex. I found the girls in my social group attractive, and I regularly attended functions where I hooked up with or dated them, and during my senior year, I met Cathy, my first love.

My father and I stayed fairly close after the divorce and I vividly recall two things about him that profoundly shaped the man I would eventually become.

Dad was a brilliant man and a loving father, but he was very "up and down" emotionally. He could be authoritative and commanding, especially when he was unhappy about something. I remember him barking orders at family members once when we were gathering for a picture. When I saw the photograph later, I realized almost nobody was actually smiling—except for me. I think I'd already learned by that time not to let my father's— or anyone's—inexplicable unhappiness color my own enjoyment of the moment.

The second thing about my dad that stuck with me was that he believed I could do better if I tried harder. During a conversation about my ninth-grade report card—which was mostly C's and B's—he said, "Well, someone needs to put the toothpaste in the tube. Looks like you may be a good candidate."

I knew that his intention wasn't to demean me but to light a fire under me to do better, and it worked. In the months and years that followed, I tried much harder in school, and my work paid off in countless ways.

That same year, I asked my school guidance counselor, Mr. Jacoby, about an intelligence test I'd taken. He said, "I can't share the actual results, but I can tell you that you were average—just average."

At this time in my life, my parents weren't involved in my education at all. While my mother somehow managed to stay on top of her very active personal, professional, and family life, she had no time to keep track of the courses all seven of us were taking, much less supervise our homework or even notice what our grades were. And she certainly didn't have money for tutors of any kind, even when it came time to prepare for the SAT and ACT college-qualifying tests.

For all those reasons, Mr. Jacoby's assessment deeply concerned me. I wondered who I would grow up to be. The guy who put toothpaste in tubes? Would I be able to support my own family one day? Because of this, I began to apply myself single-mindedly to my studies, trying so hard— perhaps *too* hard—to not be a disappointment. I wanted to impress not just my mom and dad, but the family I felt certain I was destined to have in the future.

I now know that the process for testing intelligence is deeply flawed, and that no test can evaluate your true talents and abilities. We are each born with potential that is revealed to us as our life unfolds, but at the time, it took a while for me to shake off Mr. Jacoby's comments.

You have unlimited potential for unique accomplishment contained within you; I encourage you not to let anyone persuade you otherwise. And I promise that as you continue your journey into your future, if your unique gifts have not already been revealed to you, they absolutely will be. If you need to take an intelligence test for any reason, do not be swayed—

even in the most infinitesimal way—by any negative results. Continue to steadfastly pursue your ambitions, passions, and skills until you discover your destiny.

As I entered adulthood, my ambitions were still not very specific, other than wanting to do well and be successful. But my next adventure was pivotal in helping me clarify my dreams, and it set the path my life would follow for years to come.


# 2
# GROWING UP FAST

Around the time I turned sixteen, my mother expressed concern that I was spending too much time smoking marijuana, so when I asked her permission to hitchhike around the United States that summer, she agreed, saying she "hoped it might somehow mature me."

Much to my surprise, that's exactly what happened.

I left home in July of 1973 with my friend Eric, and our thumbs were out for much of the thirty days we spent traveling. We took I-80 from Virginia to California, and then the interstate highways of the southern United States on the trip back home. Many of those who picked us up along the way had long hair, no money, a dog, and a VW bus or something similar. Seeing how they lived made me certain I didn't want to live that kind of life.

When we reached California, I decided to cut my hair short as my first step in a different direction.

Eric and I lived frugally during our journey; I began the trip with $85 in my pocket, and when I returned a month later, I still had $35.

The moment I returned, it became obvious to me and everyone around me that I had changed quite profoundly during my month on the road.

From that time forward, I kept my appearance much neater than before, and in the bedroom I shared with my older brother, I began to keep my side of the room immaculate compared to his side. I also decided to really focus on my grades and pulled my GPA up to a 3.2 by the time I graduated from high school.

Around this time, my mother told me she had a friend who was willing to sell me a used, 1964 Chevrolet Corvair for only $55 on time payments—$5 per month. But there was one condition: I could no longer smoke pot. Marijuana and other recreational drugs were no longer important to me, so I agreed without hesitation.

I entered my junior year in high school as a markedly more mature young adult, but soon discovered that my friends had not made the same choices. I felt isolated at times. We still hung around together, but I had different priorities than they did, which took me in a different direction. Eventually, this led me to college.

I started out at Northern Illinois University as a pre-veterinarian major, but quickly transferred to George Washington University because of the "C" I got in chemistry during my first semester. College was all business for me, and in truth it wasn't much fun. I had to work full-time while I was also enrolled in school full-time, majoring in political science. My parents didn't have enough savings to get me and my six brothers and sisters through college, so we each had to work, apply for scholarships and grants, and take on debt to earn our degrees.

I attended courses in the morning and early afternoon, and then worked the four-to-eleven PM shift as the evening manager at a local grocery store. After class each day, I'd dash into a vacant professor's office on campus and change into my work clothes. Thank God nobody caught me! After my shift, I'd sleepily drive home and churn through my homework before nodding off to sleep—and when the alarm went off the next morning, I'd get up and do it all again. I had no time for fraternities or a social life. In fact, I don't recall going to a single college party the whole time I was at George Washington U.

My highly focused and committed approach to life eventually led me onto that plane headed for California.

During a lunch with my father, we'd hatched the beginnings of a plan. He knew someone who could help me get a job at Lawrence Systems, a financial services firm in San Francisco. Even though all my family and friends were on the East Coast, I was excited about this new adventure. I looked forward to starting my first professional job and putting the initial part of my life behind me as I journeyed west. I figured that having a single, full-time job—without the added pressure of school—was going to be a piece of cake, compared to my college years.

I was in for a rude awakening.

My father had helped open the door to my job, so I'd skipped interviewing in person with a hiring manager. When I arrived, bright and eager, for my first day on the job, my boss asked me about the business and accounting classes I'd taken in college.

I hadn't taken *any* business or accounting classes.

Here I was, ready to fill his one open "source-document control clerk trainee" position, with a starting salary of $13,200 a year, and I was completely unprepared.

I promised I'd enroll in accounting classes at a local college at once, and was lucky he didn't fire me before I'd even started the job.

This was a much different world than the one I'd grown up in on the East Coast, where I'd been surrounded by friends and family. My life there was civil and comfortable. In San Francisco, I was on my own, and it often seemed like the Wild West to me.

One evening during my trolley ride from work to school, a man boarded and loudly announced his intention to defecate. Then he yanked his pants down and did so, right in the aisle, before taking a seat. I ran into colorful characters and disturbing incidents often during these daily rides.

Fortunately, I quickly got up to speed in accounting. After two semesters of classes (and trolley rides), my superiors became confident enough in my abilities to release me from further academic study.

One day, a colleague named Greg pulled me aside at work and told me I was not dressing appropriately. He pointed to my polyester suit and "rooster tie" (I didn't even know what a "rooster tie" was—a tie with a loud color or pattern that draws too much attention). Greg suggested I get a book called *Dress for Success*.

He also insisted I buy a wool suit and a few conservative neckties.

My father hadn't been a particularly sharp dresser, and after my parents divorced when I was in the sixth grade, I only saw him once or twice a month, and he never gave me a single word of advice on how I should dress. I bought a copy of *Dress for Success* and read it to get a sense of how my clothes could help me fit in better at my job.

I needed to more closely resemble men who were as successful as I hoped one day to be, the book said. I didn't like the idea that my clothes influenced how other people perceived me. The author contended that the right clothes might make the difference between success and failure, and that my appearance was more important than the person I was inside. While I knew in my heart and soul this wasn't true, I tried to adjust my wardrobe to look a bit more professional.

Dressing "right" wasn't the biggest challenge I faced during my early days in San Francisco. Finding housing topped that list. When I'd first arrived, I stayed briefly with Gerry, a friend of my dad's who lived outside the city, but the commute from there took far too long and I needed to find something closer to my job.

My friend Greg offered to let me stay with him while I was looking for an apartment. I showed up at his place with all my things the next evening at the time he'd told me to come, but he wasn't there, leaving me nowhere to sleep that night.

The first few motels I went to were out of my price range, but I eventually found one I could afford in an area of San Francisco known as "The Tenderloin" that was more than a little treacherous after nightfall. I slept in a motel with dirty sheets and towels for one night and then quickly moved to the old YMCA in the Embarcadero area, where my room was tiny but clean, with a shared, community-style bathroom down the hall. Weeks later, I finally managed to find a decent apartment I could afford.

"This too shall pass" became my new mantra, and to this day, those words go through my mind when challenges loom in my life. I encourage you to adopt a similar perspective, so your own challenges don't bog you down. In order to navigate to the best possible resolution, you need to address things calmly and clearly, keeping your full faculties and focus at the ready. This approach continues to be a powerful and effective tool for me.

Unfortunately, more challenges lay ahead.

## 3

# NAVIGATING THE RECESSION

In 1979, the global economic recession began to rock the financial services industry. Lawrence Systems, where I worked, was a collateral management company. We would hold the inventory, accounts receivable, and documents pledged by companies as collateral for bank loans. With bank loan rates skyrocketing, companies were doing everything they could to try to lower their loan rates and fees. Lawrence Systems was caught in the middle of this scramble, and we were forced to lay off many of our seasoned employees.

The high-salaried senior staff in our investment banking group were the first to get their notices, so the company needed less expensive employees to quickly fill those positions. I had only been on the internal audit desk for a few months, but I'd won the confidence of my superiors, and while advanced accounting was still beyond me, I had developed a nose for the collateral management business. Because of this, the company rapidly moved me up—first to an outside auditing position, and then to oversee region-wide assignments, including the entire West Coast and Hawaii.

During this period, I first met Rich Norum, who would later become my partner when we cofounded our first company, ENS. When Rich became a member of my team at Lawrence Systems, he quickly proved himself to be one of the brightest guys in the office, so I asked him to take charge of key audit functions. He was enormously helpful with the "problem" accounts. Rich had no problem taking a straight-forward approach and a firm stand with business owners when needed, and he became my trusted assistant.

The most challenging duty we had was called "locking up" an account. The stories that led to this action were often the same. The owner of a company would be splurging on a more extravagant lifestyle than he could afford, so he would start to fudge the business's collateral balances. He'd inflate inventory or other collateral so he could draw on a larger loan balance, which allowed him to continue his out-of-control personal spending…until the company got caught. Our audits were always unannounced, so it was only a matter of time before we noticed. In one case, the owner collected polo horses. Others had private jets and several luxurious residences.

Once a year, I flew to the Hawaiian islands to audit our accounts there. I was born in Hawaii and always jumped at the chance to go back. During one of these Maui trips, as I was tooling around the west side of the island just before dusk, I noticed the sun was about to set behind the islands in the distance. I pulled over, turned up the radio, and marveled at the breathtaking spectacle before me. Everything was going so well in my life, and I felt like I was in heaven.

Since that day, I've made it a point to stop as often as I can and appreciate the sunset or other moments of striking beauty around me. I connect these sights to a deep sense of Divine presence in the natural world. They give me inspiration and grounding in my day-to-day life, regardless of what might be happening in my personal or business world.

I suggest you, too, keep your eyes open for marvels in the natural world that surrounds your own life. These sights can help you to feel a deeper connection and remind you there's a grander force at work in the universe, of which you are a part. This is the best way I've found to stay clear and grounded as the tectonic plates of my life shift and push me in new and unexpected directions.

One of those shifts was about to take place.

# PART 2

A New Direction

# 4
# A LESSON LEARNED THE HARD WAY

In late 1982, something happened that changed my life forever.

One Saturday morning, as I was getting my apartment organized, I got a call from my sister Maureen. I was near the middle of seven siblings, with two older and four younger, and Maureen had been born right after me.

"Steve! I'm getting married. Will you come to my wedding in June?"

"Maureen, wow! You're getting married! You wouldn't believe how busy I am and I'm not sure I can take that weekend off. Let me get back to you, okay?"

Maureen sounded disappointed but hopeful. I promised I'd call her within the next month to let her know.

That night, I had a shocking dream in which Maureen had died. It felt real and incredibly scary. I woke up so shaken that I wanted to call her immediately, but it was still the middle of the night. The next morning, my heart was racing as I dialed her number. It felt like a full minute passed between each ring.

When Maureen answered at last, I breathed a joyful sigh of relief and said, "Maureen, I'm so sorry I didn't say this yesterday, but I wouldn't miss your wedding for anything in the world!"

The months passed quickly, and before I knew it, I was flying back to Virginia and the home I grew up in, where Maureen's wedding and reception would be held. On June 26, 1983, Maureen and her husband David joyfully took their vows. Everyone had a marvelous time. Someone took a picture of Maureen, my younger brother Dennis, and me, with Maureen in the middle. We all had ear-to-ear smiles.

That was the last time I ever saw her.

A few short months later, my older brother Kevin called to tell me that Maureen and David had been in a terrible accident. While driving home late the night before, she had dozed off at the wheel. The car had spun out of control and flipped over, and because Maureen was not wearing a seat belt, the crash broke her neck, killing her instantly. Her husband, who was asleep and belted in the back seat, survived unscathed.

I flew back to Virginia, this time for the funeral. While I was heartbroken, I could also sense that something important in me had changed.

I spent the next few months trying to process my sister's death and the effect it had on me spiritually. At a deep level, I had felt close to God for a long time and had unconsciously been placing trust in God to guide me in everything I did. I grew up in a Catholic home and had served as an altar boy, but it was not the authoritarian God of the Catholic church I had gotten close to—it was the loving God I'd felt in my heart from the time I was a child.

Throughout my upbringing and into my adult life, I'd always sensed the presence of this unconditionally loving God. I believed God guided me in the big decisions I'd made in my life. I now knew something Divine had visited my sleep months earlier, on the night I dreamed of Maureen's death. God was making sure I went to the wedding so I could share the precious moments I had with her before she passed. I can't imagine how I would have felt if I'd missed the wedding and that time with her.

Up to that point in my life, I'd been pursuing my business success fervently, but, as I've mentioned, something had shifted following my sister's passing. I became more cautious from that time forward, never again losing track of what was truly important to me. I understood clearly now that I could win material success in life but still be a loser by missing out on something far more important—the time I spent with those I loved.

I encourage you to stay clear about what is most important to you, too, and to let that clarity be the filter through which you consider taking actions of any kind. It's so easy to become caught up in the momentum of our lives that we don't always realize how far we've gotten off track until we miss out on valuable experiences, and by then it can be hard to get back on our destiny path.

My sister's passing was a "wake up and smell the coffee" moment for me. It seemed to be more of a sign to slow down rather than to stop or change course.

Despite this, not too far ahead, my path was about to veer sharply in a new direction.

# 5
# CHOOSING TRAINING OVER FINANCIAL WEALTH

When I returned home to San Francisco after the funeral, I had to decide about my career. The recession of 1980 to1983 had been punishing for the banking industry. Interest rates were in the mid to high teens, even exceeding 20 percent at one point. Companies did everything they could to reduce their loan balances and fees. Since our fees at Lawrence Systems came on top of loan interest fees, banks came under incredible pressure to reduce or drop our services.

I knew my opportunities in this field were limited, so I started an intensive search for another job, eventually landing on two practical options. The fast-growing San Jose office for Coldwell Banker Commercial Real Estate was interested in hiring me, and I believed that the San Francisco office for IBM's National Accounts Division would also extend me an offer.

19

Commercial real estate offered an opportunity for quick wealth—but at IBM, I'd have a chance to receive top-notch training.

In the end, I felt guided to the job that offered more training. On some level, I recognized the value of a source of income that would also help me improve my business skills, so I could operate at a higher organizational level.

In December of 1983, I became a sales trainee at IBM. This meant I was back down at the bottom rung of the office ladder. IBM quickly shipped me out to their training center for the National Accounts Division in Irving, Texas.

I'm a people person, so I enjoyed the interaction with my instructors and classmates at the training center, but I was not the most polished salesperson. During one of my classes, an instructor said, "Not everyone is meant to make it to the top. Be happy with what comes to you, and you'll enjoy your career."

His advice reminded me of my father's parting words when he and I had lunch at the airport, all those years ago. He'd said he would see me "at the top." But would I ever make it to the top?

Next, my sales manager in San Francisco told me I would be able to reach the level of a director at the company but no higher. The situation reminded me of my discouraging early days at Lawrence Systems. I felt right at home.

In spite of the glass ceiling that had appeared above me, IBM gave me a break: they invited me to give the lead presentation to announce the new AS400 mini-computer in San Francisco. This was an important announcement, and with 2,000 people expected to attend, I'd be speaking before the biggest audience of my career thus far. I spent hours memorizing my speech.

While my presentation went well, I knew I'd invested way too much time preparing for it, so I decided to enroll in Dale Carnegie and Toastmasters to improve my extemporaneous speaking skills. I hoped this training would help me create more effective speeches with less prep time, knowing those skills would be invaluable to me in everything I did professionally for the rest of my life.

I'm sharing this part of my story with you because it illustrates how single events can wind up being turning points in your life that move you further ahead on your path. Regardless of the direction you have taken up until now, never tell yourself you can't get where you want to go because you don't feel equipped or prepared to make such a shift. In fact, everything you've experienced so far might already have made you more ready than you realize.

To further illustrate this: IBM soon assigned me to a major account where a large sales team oversaw computer mainframe devices. Then, when IBM bought the Rolm technology company, I moved over to lead the voice/data integration team.

This was during the late 1980s, when technology was transforming the way businesses managed global communications. Companies were replacing their typewriters with desktop computers for the first time, and we were right in the middle of it!

I could never have guessed how handy my prior experience was about to become.

# 6
# A PREMONITION

When I first moved to California, the only people I knew there were my father's friend Gerry and my grandparents, and my grandparents moved east shortly after my arrival. Because I was so incredibly busy with my career, it was quite a while before I developed an active social life.

In the early 1980s, I met a woman who was special enough to start a close relationship with. She had grown up just south of San Francisco in San Mateo. After dating for a few years, we were married in 1985. Unfortunately, neither of us had figured out who we were yet, so we had no business making a lifetime commitment to each other. A little more than a year later, we divorced.

During these early years, I moved around the San Francisco Bay area to sample the various unique communities and the unique weather that came with them. Mark Twain famously described the weather in parts of San Francisco in this way: "The coldest winter I've ever spent was my summer in San Francisco."

I liked the Marina District in San Francisco and Marin County best and ended up purchasing my first townhouse condominium in Marin County overlooking the San Francisco Bay. This location gave me access to good places to run, hike, and ride my mountain bike with friends.

During this time, I got to know John, a trader for an investment bank based in San Francisco. He was talented at his profession and quite successful. John was involved in philanthropy in the city and had even started his own annual charitable auction.

John would sometimes say, "In another life, I'd like to be a social activist and really put it all on the line." He clearly felt inspired to do more. I recall thinking, *Why wait until another life? Why not do it now?* I can see now that this was a premonition of what was to happen in my own life.

If you've ever felt you'd like to be engaged in something more meaningful in your own day-to-day pursuits, take a close look at those feelings—not years from now, but right away. Time is one of the most wonderful gifts we have, but we don't get an unlimited supply. Stay alert for any opportunities for growth that come your way.

IBM offered continuing free education to its employees, so I signed up for something called the "President's Class," which they created to show students what it's like to be the president of a company. Our lessons included a description of an "entrepreneur"—someone willing to organize a new venture involving considerable initiative and risk so a new endeavor might be created.

I became instantly captivated by this idea and decided I would become an entrepreneur. Now I knew what I wanted to do next, but I had no idea how to get started.

I liked training and working with my brilliant colleagues at IBM, but I didn't enjoy the politics that went with being part of a large organization. I considered a variety of different ideas for my next move, but the one that excited me most was business communications.

Rich Norum, who had been my trusted assistant at Lawrence Systems, now worked for a technology innovator in Plano, Texas. He'd become an expert in emerging technologies in the business communications field, and since I'd worked with new, high-speed technologies on the sales side at IBM, we'd stayed connected as friends who shared similar interests.

Our occasional chats convinced us that, taken together, we had a huge inventory of skills in designing and implementing new, high-speed communications systems. The combination of our individual talents might be more than the sum of its parts.

We began talking seriously about starting our own firm.

Rich and I spent the next year doing research and planning. We interviewed others who had launched their own companies in our field, and we attended trade shows where we picked the brains of other entrepreneurs and industry experts. We then strategized about the products we could offer, and we even set up a small line of credit with a bank.

Finally, we felt ready to take the big leap we'd been building toward. We quit our stable jobs and together formed the company that would become Enterprise Networking Systems (ENS).

Everything in my life was about to change.

# 7
# TASTING THE DREAM

On January 1st, 1990, Rich and I invested in some used office furniture and moved into our small executive suite. Rich handed me the business cards he'd designed for us. His said, "Network Integration Manager," as he would manage the engineering and operations. My card said "Marketing Director," as my responsibilities were sales, marketing, and the overall leadership of the company.

We were off and running.

When we left our technology jobs, our co-workers wondered about the choice we were making in leaving secure careers, and our families were concerned about our ability to pull it off and be successful. They hoped for the best, but we could sense their reservations. Start-ups had not yet become fashionable, and everyone thought we might be making a big mistake. I rented out my back bedroom to help pay my mortgage, and I cashed out some of my IRA to assist with the bills for the first six months.

We had very little financial room to maneuver, so Rich and I created an operating budget with a big goal and a firm deadline: Our new business would generate $240,000 in sales in the first six months and $800,000 in the first year, or we'd give up and go back to work for an established company.

On our first day, my mom called to wish me the best. She wanted me to know she still believed in me by sharing her enthusiasm and support. She also sent a plant for the office.

We launched the company with just the two of us, working seven-day weeks to stay on top of sales, tech support, and administrative functions. At six months, we were short of the target we'd set—but we were close. At six months and two weeks, we shot past the target and began hiring employees. By year's end, our revenue exceeded a million dollars.

When we cofounded ENS, I hadn't been sure I could really do everything required to make it a success. I didn't know if I had the "right stuff" to recruit others and be a good leader. Engineers and technical professionals were in demand and could work where they pleased, making it harder to find and entice the best ones to join with us. I understood that I'd need to stretch and grow to make this venture work, and knew I had to accept that, like our company, I, too, was a "work in progress."

Rich and I had felt like high-wire walkers without a safety net during the company's first year, but we'd put in the necessary effort to nail our goal. As the year ended, we felt comfortable enough to breathe, at least a little.

We were getting our first taste of what our society and our culture had taught us about success. We were measuring our progress based on profit from what we were *doing*. Much later, I became aware that it is what we are *being* in the world that brings true fulfillment, and this realization completely redefined "success" for me.

As I suggested earlier, I hope that walking you through my story allows you to see aspects of yourself and of your own longings. If so, I also hope

I can guide you to a similar path to the one I followed that led me from a focus on *external* measures of success to *internal* measures that are much more lasting, meaningful, and true.

Let me tell you more about how I got there.

# 8
# THE INVENTION THAT
# CHANGED EVERYTHING

Entrepreneurial opportunities are often born on the back of new *market* trends, and fulfillment opportunities are often carried in the heart of new *thought* trends. We are living in a time when people are thinking in new ways about the real meaning of life and the true purpose of our existence.

It's not by happenstance that both aspects of life—new market trends and new thought trends—joined together to carry me toward a shift in my life's focus. This might also be what carries you to that sense of fulfillment and meaningful expression for which your heart yearns.

Rich and I could not have known then that a once-in-a-lifetime trend was about to redefine life as we knew it, including how we get our news, how we meet other people, how we work, shop, educate ourselves, and so much more.

It all began with the advent of the personal computer. In the mid to late 1980s, homes and businesses started buying personal computers in larger numbers. This groundswell turned into a tidal wave by the 1990s when the internet was born. Together, the PC and the Internet empowered people in both their personal and business lives. Computer users felt liberated in ways they'd never experienced before because they had instant access to friends, colleagues, and vendors on the other side of town, across the country, and around the world.

Before the Internet and personal computers, most large businesses used what were known as "dumb terminals" connected to mainframe computers. The goal was to maximize the number of terminals that a single mainframe could manage. At that time, more than 17,000 terminals could be connected to a single IBM central processor.

But before long, the personal computer revolution brought the power of that mainframe to your desk. Creating graphics and spreadsheets, comparing colors and fonts, and experimenting with subtle design changes were suddenly things *anyone* could easily learn to do. However, communication links were stuck where they'd started out, with large, thick, slow-speed cables connecting local devices.

Eventually users demanded faster access to everything, which drove innovation in the form of the thin, flexible, high-speed communication links—but those wouldn't surface until years later. As the first wave of computer use swept over the world, PCs and connecting devices were rapidly filling up every available space with the bulky equipment needed to support local, campus, and global communications.

This created a torrent of demand for communication systems supporting PC environments. "Client server" networks started springing up and inventors raced to create innovative technologies to support campus and remote communications. As fast as a new device appeared, it would be overtaken by the rising demand from users who pushed for higher network speeds.

The "network effect" of computers was drawing more users in, and these users were producing content, creating websites, and requesting services. The escalation of users and services was exponential, and the growth curve went hyperbolic.

In the early days, computer services were often unreliable, due to the sheer strain of constant growth. Technology could not keep up. Large businesses with thousands of users had trouble finding devices that could be counted on to support their local and wide-area communications. This was a nightmare for businesses trying to stay competitive and relevant— but a boon for what Rich and I were aiming to do. We were very much at the right time and in the right place, too.

Silicon Valley is roughly forty-five square miles, and our South San Francisco office was within easy driving distance of the whole of the valley, which was becoming the birthplace for the technology companies that would lead the Internet revolution. Devices called hubs, routers, and switches were being invented and produced at a breakneck pace to support communications between PCs and other devices.

Entrepreneurial opportunities are about solving problems. Entrepreneurs strive to create order out of chaos. Our company, Enterprise Networking Systems (ENS), supplied exactly that—solving problems through organization. We helped large companies plan, design, and implement secure, high-speed communication systems across enterprise networks.

When Rich and I started ENS, our goal wasn't making a great deal of money; it was building a great company. I had already begun to feel a shift from "doing" to "being" as my life's focus. When we got a new customer, it felt personal. We took our time to meticulously plan and build a strong, secure, high-performance network to perfectly suit each client's needs. Word spread of our hands-on approach, and our network integration business rapidly took off.

We were developing a reputation as a company that businesses could trust to compare and obtain innovative technology, then install it and support it, taking time to understand the unique business requirements of each client along the way.

We soon needed to hire more people to keep up with orders. We needed to find employees who were as good or better than we were in the areas the two of us had been covering, such as sales, engineering, operations, and marketing. The right hires would be able to take certain things off our plates, leaving us the time for other things needing our attention.

When Rich and I started ENS, we were in our early thirties and not seasoned managers, and we made mistakes. We also learned a lot about recruiting a team that was aligned with our values, and then leading them to the levels of success that lay ahead of us in the near distance. From this, I began to experience, for the first time, the sense of being aligned with my values within myself, and I began exploring more deeply the question of what could bring the highest level of meaning and purpose to my life.

This is a question I encourage you to consider regularly in your own life. Taking the time for focused soul-searching is a critical part of creating alignment with your deeper, foundational beliefs and dreams. This is the first step in discovering a fulfilling answer.

# 9
# THE BALANCING ACT OF BUSINESS SUCCESS

As my personal explorations deepened during this phase of getting ENS off the ground, I realized that my friends had no idea how difficult it was to start a business. I remember one telling me, "You are so lucky. When the weather is nice, you can just decide to go for a mountain bike ride or a hike! You can plan something fun instead of having to go to work."

Unfortunately, nothing could have been further from the truth at that time. Their ideas about me and my career made me examine what I was doing in my life—as opposed to what they *thought* I was doing.

In truth, my life had become a balancing act between success and failure. We needed to reach weekly and monthly sales goals to keep the company afloat and move forward. If I didn't meet those goals every week, I'd topple off that wire, the business would fail, and I'd need to find a regular job and start all over. Fear of failure gave me a tremendous incentive to go to work each day and make things happen. That left precious little time for hiking and biking!

To help me perform at my best, I'd get up at five a.m. and hit the gym on the way to work. That regular morning regimen helped me build the stamina and mental strength I needed to carry me through the long work days.

Thankfully, that hard work was paying off and we were making steady progress on generating new accounts, as growing a business like ours required a lot of cash flow.

In our first five years, we not only moved five times, each time to a larger office space, but skilled engineers and sales people in the data communications industry needed to be well-compensated. Our engineers earned six-figure salaries, and sales people could potentially earn over $200K and $300K due to commissions.

We were grateful we were able to recruit so many talented team members, and keep them happy enough that we had very little employee turnover.

# 10
# OUR GROUNDBREAKING COMPANY CULTURE

One way we kept our employees happy and loyal to us when they had so many other options in the job market was our company culture. ENS was committed to serving our customers and the local community, not only delivering what we promised to our clients, but often over-delivering. We tried to exceed expectations and support long-term business relationships.

Inside ENS, we made sure the work environment was free from any kind of office politics or drama. Rich and I were just as committed to our team members as we were to our clients.

Because we also strongly believed businesses should contribute to the surrounding community, we decided to pitch in to help local schools and non-profits. One of our first ventures into this effort came when we adopted South San Francisco High School, which was near our first office. We supplied the hubs, routers, and support services to get their computer network up and running, without cost to them.

Other, larger technology companies also got involved in this kind of charity work, but they often asked for public statements of support from those they helped. We were only interested in doing good. We'd simply go in, get the work done, and not ask for anything in return.

Our prospective employees and clients noticed these things. We developed a reputation for unparalleled customer support; offered a merit-based work environment; and supplied much needed community support. All of this put us in a solid position to win new accounts and recruit top talent. People wanted to work with us and for us.

31

As the company grew, we were able to expand into Southern California and even the mid-Atlantic region on the East Coast.

Rich and I drew modest salaries, earning much less than we paid our top-performing employees. This helped us build up the large cash reserve we could use to lease larger offices, pay new hires, and cover the expenses needed to grow into new geographies.

This focus away from the highest personal gain to the highest good for the largest number helped me to know *experientially* that the highest good for the largest number was indeed also the highest good for me, because what serves The Whole inevitably serves every *part* of The Whole.

This foundational awareness would have a profound impact on my choices in the years ahead—but at that time, new and unexpected adventures and learning experiences still awaited me around every corner.

A small (at the time) company called Cisco Systems had become an early leader in the networking technology field. They supplied the backbone communications systems for campus and global networks. They faced rivals, of course, but soon Cisco became the technology of choice for most international companies. And rather than make their products available through integrators like our company, Cisco preferred to sell directly to customers. Their approach was quite successful.

By coincidence, my girlfriend at that time invited me to attend an alumni event on the Cisco campus where the chairman and CEO, John Morgridge, was to make a speech. During his presentation, he made it abundantly clear that they did not favor working with partners and had no plans to do so anytime soon.

"We have the dominant position in networking technology," he said, "and we intend to grow our presence in global accounts by sourcing and supporting our equipment directly. We believe our direct relationship is a competitive advantage."

I was dumbfounded when, a few months later, John Chambers—the head of sales for Cisco at the time—called to ask for a meeting with me. By this time, ENS occupied a 1,200-square-foot office on a higher floor in the same building where we'd had our original, two-person office. But we were still "small potatoes" in the world of Cisco enterprise accounts. Our chief advantage was that we were well-regarded by major accounts in California. On a few occasions, we'd even beat Cisco in head-to-head competitions for clients.

John was a powerful, broad-shouldered man who exuded confidence. I'd seen him speak and was always impressed. Upon arrival, he didn't waste any time before inspecting our office and meeting the staff. He didn't seem to mind that we were a small company. "I like you guys," he said. "We don't work with integrators and don't even have contracts to formally support you, but we've decided to partner with you going forward."

Rich and I were stunned but ecstatic. We knew a partnership with Cisco would be a game-changer for us. I tried to restrain my excitement as I told John we were interested in accepting his offer. We sealed the deal with a simple handshake and he headed out the door. Just that quickly, the course of our business lives had changed forever.

Like our earlier IBM partnership, this relationship rapidly increased the size of our business. Many large companies preferred the extra service we offered in designing multi-vendor networks, as well as the ongoing support we provided after installation. New clients began hiring us at a furious pace.

The life lesson here for us (and I hope for you, too) was to never allow any worst-case scenario about the future to overwhelm us. We should always remain open to the possibility that a totally unexpected turn of events might flip a "negative" into a "positive" in the blink of an eye.

What I learned from this remarkable aspect of on-the-ground life has served me well in countless ways ever since. It was especially vital when I later contemplated life-altering decisions to help bring more meaning and a higher purpose to the work I do.

# 11
# A PERSONAL AND PROFESSIONAL VISION

It was around this time that I also decided to take on a new roommate in my two-bedroom Marin townhouse. I ran a classified ad in the county newspaper, and quickly attracted a promising prospect. Jeff was in his late twenties, well-educated, wise beyond his years, and was also connected to numerous successful and up-and-coming entrepreneurs in Silicon Valley circles, so I agreed to let him move into my back bedroom.

One day, Jeff mentioned that an international group called the Young Entrepreneurs' Organization (YEO) was forming to support young entrepreneurs. Neil Balter, the founder of California Closets, was the international chairman and was going to be coming to San Francisco to launch a new chapter.

I attended the meeting and was excited to meet other entrepreneurs leading fast-growing businesses.

One of the things that most attracted me to YEO was the wide range of personality types in the membership—from outgoing, well-spoken athletes to shy, introverted tech nerds, and everything in between. It made me realize that success didn't primarily depend on your personality. Success was also a matter of selecting the right industry, finding the correct business model, and putting together a solid team—and then nurturing a supportive culture in your company and committing to an effective growth path.

These lessons were useful to me later when I removed myself from the search for "success" through business and chose to focus on what I've come to think of as a New Universal Dream. I redefined my idea of success in life, and my focus became service to others and to the world (of which I am an integral part). I was determined to live as my bigger, "authentic" self, rather than my smaller, self-interested self.

I've learned so much about every aspect of life by simply hearing about the experiences of others—and that is what you are doing right now by reading this book. Here, for example, is a wonderful insight I picked up in mid-1993, when a friend in the Young Entrepreneurs' Organization put me in touch with Bob Metcalf, one of the founders of 3Com, a pioneering company in the networking field.

Shortly after retiring from 3Com, Bob had imagined his life to be in thirds: one third growing up and academically preparing for a career; one third creating a successful, professional career; and one third giving back through philanthropic endeavors.

I felt instantly drawn to this idea and wanted to pick Bob's brain for more suggestions. He agreed to speak with me by phone and was glad to know I was interested in emulating his "thirds" approach to life. I came away from the call deeply inspired to start envisioning my own path to that same way of living—focusing particular attention on the final third of Bob's formula, which was about giving back to the world.

# 12
# FINDING MY SOULMATE

During those early ENS years, I was still single, although I dated a couple of interesting women. One was the Harvard MBA who had taken me to the alumni dinner at the Cisco campus; another was an attorney at an up-and-coming San Francisco law firm. Both were bright and pretty, but I saw signs that they were attracted to me because of *what* I was, not *who* I was.

One day, the attorney even caught me off-guard when she said, "I never thought I'd be with a Goldilocks guy who can't even tell a dirty joke from time to time." I realized she was teasing me for being too nice, but her comment made it clear that she didn't really appreciate me for being me. She seemed to prefer a man who looked at the world in a more cynical and jaded way, with a sardonic sense of humor to match. I had no interest in being that kind of man.

This and other clues made me face the reality that we were not a good match, so I stopped seeing her and began dating women who seemed to appreciate who I am on the inside—not just my professional status. Before that time, I'd never given much thought to finding the perfect woman for me. Now, I decided that the next woman I dated seriously would have to be wholesome, good-hearted, and generous.

I was also getting a sense that I needed a life partner who was deeply spiritual. This feeling was a little bewildering at that time. While I'd felt close to God my whole life, and considered myself to be a spiritual person, an overarching spiritual focus didn't really fit with my position as the CEO of a rapidly-growing Silicon Valley company. I was on the fast track to fulfilling my dreams of personal success as I then defined them. But of course, I had no idea what lay ahead of me on the not-so-distant horizon.

Our third hire during the ENS years was a smart, attractive young woman named Stephanie Monroe whom we recruited to aid with marketing. She also was open to jumping in and helping with anything when we needed her. Her desk was just across from my glass-windowed office, so I saw her every day as I sat at my desk. I often thought, *What a nice, good-hearted woman she is.*

It wasn't long before I realized I wanted to ask her out, but I knew dating might be awkward while she was my employee. I asked my friends what they thought. They were unanimous in suggesting I start by spending time with her at business lunches.

"Keep it safe and platonic until you get to know her," everyone said. They advised me to make sure I was serious about wanting to spend the rest of my life with her before we began dating—as if *that* didn't exponentially increase the pressure of the whole situation!

I already enjoyed Stephanie's company. She was hardworking, creative, and one of the most wholesome women I'd ever met. She never engaged in gossip and seemed to believe in the goodness of people. It was clear that she always tried to do her best. She was the first to offer help. I don't remember ever hearing her say anything mean-spirited about anyone.

Fortunately, we had marketing plans needing attention at the office, so it wasn't at all suspicious when I asked Stephanie if we could plan some working lunches to focus on them. Over the months of lunches that followed, I became more comfortable with the idea that she was "the one" for me.

I could tell that Stephanie was a spiritual person, but not in any obvious way. She never seemed eager to talk about her faith and beliefs. I learned that, despite her openness and her big heart, she was very private about deeply personal things. This is an approach I later came to think of as "Oprah spirituality." Her spirituality showed more in actions than in words.

At one of our working lunches, I asked her an out-of-the-blue question: How many children did she want to have? She gave me a funny look, and I could tell she was starting to become suspicious of my motives. It was time for me to either ask her out on a date or take a step back. Everything in me told me to move forward.

I invited her to join me for dinner at the Waterfront Restaurant in San Francisco one evening. She said yes.

At the restaurant, I was going to ask her if she thought it was awkward for us to eat at a fancy restaurant like this, thinking she'd say "yes." That would give me an opening to tell her I had romantic feelings for her. Unfortunately, she said it *wasn't* awkward. Yet I could tell she was as nervous as I was. I realized suddenly that, after all the months of build-up, this dinner would be harder than I'd thought.

We made it through the first couple of courses, but the tension continued to grow. Just before the entree arrived, I somehow managed to blurt out my romantic intentions. I shared that she was special, I wanted to date her and we could go slow. The moment I did, a wide smile spread across her face—a smile I will never forget.

As we left the Waterfront restaurant that night and walked across the parking lot to our cars, I felt so happy with how things had gone that I stopped and turned to Stephanie. We looked into each other's eyes and then kissed for the first time. Then we smiled at each other and went to our separate cars.

It was one of the most magical moments of my life.

We still celebrate the anniversary of that wonderful evening on June 10 every year. That was the day we decided to move our relationship to the next level.

Stephanie told me later that the first call she'd made when she got home was to her mother to share what had happened between us. The fact that she was in such a hurry to tell her mother about us, after just one kiss, told me the step we were taking was just as big for her as it was for me.

The next challenging part came the following day, when I sat our ENS team down to share that Stephanie and I were going to begin dating. Our CFO asked when Stephanie would be leaving the company. As it turned out, Stephanie had already thought about this and had been planning to leave if our relationship ever turned this particular corner. Somehow, we made our relationship work without a hitch, so it never came to that.

We dated for five years before getting married in October of 1997, at which time she officially resigned as an employee.

# 13
# INVESTING IN THE FUTURE

Near the end of 1994, we reached a new high mark in sales. We had plenty to feel good about. But trouble was just around the corner.

At this time in our ENS journey, Rich and I each owned 50 percent of the company, and our board of directors consisted of just the two of us. We decided to bring others into the fold who might be willing to contribute their vision, wisdom, and insight to our continuing growth process. To this end, we created a board of advisors. The board had no financial or management responsibilities; they were all friends whom I respected. The board's sole purpose was to offer advice and guidance.

Members of this board included an executive from a commodity network supplier, a senior real estate executive, an executive from the Pacific Stock Exchange, and a venture capital executive. Our updates were brief and, in retrospect, inadequate, so our new advisors never really got a good sense of the breadth of our opportunities or challenges. Because we offered them no income or equity in the company, they didn't have any real reason to invest their time by digging in to help guide us.

Our 1994 end-of-year board of advisors meeting was in Union Square in San Francisco. Rich, Stephanie, and I drove up to the meeting together. We were sure there would be good news, so we planned an ENS team meeting later in the day to celebrate our successes.

During the advisor's meeting, we updated the board on our growth and our vision for more of the same. The commodity network supplier executive jumped in at this point.

"You don't really have a sustainable business. Networking equipment is heading toward commoditization, and soon the engineering services you offer will no longer be necessary." I was stunned. He predicted that our margins (the difference between cost and sales price) would rapidly deteriorate and threaten our financial viability.

To my amazement, the other executives—who had little knowledge of our industry—agreed with him.

Our meeting with our ENS team later in the day would not be celebrational. I wanted to be honest with them about what the board of advisors had said, but I also didn't want to deflate their enthusiasm about the company's future. "It didn't go as well as I'd planned," I told them. "One of our advisors feels the future technology trends might limit our growth and financial strength."

The ENS team couldn't help but feel deflated by the executive's assessment, but this turned out to be the least of our problems. Soon afterwards, Rich came to me and announced that he'd decided he wanted to leave the company. He asked me to buy out his interest. We discussed this possibility at length and decided to continue growing the company until its value would make the buyout price he wanted more manageable.

In the meantime, we continued to work together. But knowing he wanted to leave created an element of strain in our relationship.

The Internet was going through explosive growth in the mid-1990s. An Internet summit planned for New York City caught my attention. This new global system of interconnected computer networks was one of the huge drivers of my company's growth, so I thought I'd better attend.

Jim Clark with Netscape and Steve Case with America Online (AOL) were among those presenting. It was fascinating listening to Clark share about Netscape's plans, but the most powerful moments for me came from listening to Case's speech. Executives from well-known tech companies Compuserv and Prodigy shared the stage with Case at one point. I felt Case's vision for the industry—and AOL in particular—was unparalleled. He absolutely blew my mind.

After the conference, I felt so positive AOL would be wildly successful, I decided to buy stock in the company. Then I tried to convince Stephanie to do the same. Unfortunately, she was not an easy sell on the idea. She had the whole of her $15,000 savings invested in a financial guaranty insurance, a bond-like instrument that made small payments each year. She couldn't bear the thought that she might lose her investment.

I guaranteed it for her, promising I'd pay her back if any of her investment was lost. We invested $7,500 in AOL; by 1999, that investment had grown to $1.2 million. We also invested $7,500 in a software company that made excellent profits over time. We moved this profit into an account that became the financial basis for the charitable work we continue to do today.

Before we invested in AOL, a venture capitalist I respected had warned me that the Internet might fizzle out. I was sure he was wrong. In the years that followed, industry after industry was disrupted as entrepreneurs sprinted to create digital companies that could deliver a better product faster and for less money. This explosive new trend fueled our growth at ENS, as companies were constantly upgrading their backbone networks and adding performance and security features. In 1995 and 1997, *INC.* magazine put ENS on the "*INC.* 500" list of America's fastest-growing private companies.

The main problem with breakneck growth is there is little room for error. Any glitch in hiring, training, finding new office space, or the loss of a major account can seriously challenge a growing organization like ours. A case in point: While Stephanie and I were vacationing in Hawaii, Rich called to tell me that one of ENS' top sales representatives had decided to quit without notice. Not only was the timing bad, with me out of town, but this sales rep had been responsible for some of our larger accounts. I knew they would need special attention to transition to a new rep.

Since we were already on overload, this setback meant longer days— and we were already putting in full days and weeks.

Instead of enjoying my vacation, I pondered these issues in our hotel room on the Big Island of Hawaii.

# 14
# CONVERSATIONS WITH... GOD

In the summer of 1995, my mother called me one day and said, "You must read a book called *Conversations with God: Book 1,* by Neale Donald Walsch. Your sister Kathy says it's going to change your whole life."

Her suggestion couldn't have come at a worse time. ENS was consuming all my waking hours, and I certainly wasn't looking for something new to read! And the thought of a book changing "my whole life" wasn't appealing.

I was living my version of personal success; why would I want *anything* to change, much less *everything*?

Fortunately, my mother and sister continued to try to persuade me, and I went out a week later and picked it up from a nearby bookstore. From the first pages of this wonderful book—to my complete astonishment—the loving God I'd felt connected to for my whole life came fully alive.

Everything I'd always held to be true was there: God loves us unconditionally. We were never meant to fear God. We are never judged. We are supported always. So much of this profound wisdom was new to me, but it resonated deeply, as if I'd been in touch with this wisdom, as a felt experience, the whole of my life.

The book explained what it truly means for God to be omnipresent, omniscient, and omnipotent, and what it means for God to be physicalized as spirit offspring, the Earth, and even surrounding life. The book's recurring theme that "We Are All One" suggests that everything and everyone is of God and inseparable from God.

God and life are synonymous, so life in every form is sacred. The ocean is a good metaphor for this relationship. God, the Divine, is the ocean; Each of us, the planet, and all of life are the waves. We live, move, and have our being in the ocean, even when we land upon the shore, because we still recede back into the ocean.

Why are we here? God in the book answers: "To live as the expression of the Divine that we are, mindful that our true nature is God's nature because there is no separation. This is how we have everlasting life and unlimited potential, and this is why love is truly our essence. It is in our DNA."

At the time, *Conversations with God, Book 1* was already on the *New York Times* bestseller list and would remain there for 137 weeks. People around the world deeply resonated with God's messages. Our planet was facing so many challenges; it made sense that God would want to give humanity greater clarity now. God would want to give us steps we could take to course-correct and overcome those challenges, to create the sustainable future that surely was part of the plan for our existence on the Earth. Neale's book was the vehicle for that message.

That first day I opened the book, I read for nearly an hour. Then I raced in to tell Stephanie what I'd read. I could tell she was a little taken aback at first, but she seemed to tune in to my passion and listened intently.

Stephanie smiled and said she looked forward to reading it when I was done—which she did. And while it didn't completely transform her outlook on life, as it had mine, she also soon read Deepak Chopra's *Seven Spiritual Laws of Success* and Gary Zukav's *Seat of the Soul.* Both of those books expressed similar views about the nature of human existence, and they seemed to speak more deeply to her.

It was clear from our conversations that we now shared an aligned vision of the emerging new spirituality and the impact it would have on our lives.

During the three years we'd been together, we hadn't been overtly religious in most aspects of our lives, though we still considered ourselves Christians and often attended the Menlo Park Presbyterian Church near us on Sundays, a practice that continued even as our feelings about the world and what was important began to shift.

The very week my mother first told me I had to buy *Conversations with God*, I'd been contemplating a spiritual question that had occurred to me while I was reading the Bible. I realized the Bible didn't explain why God would ask us to be blindly obedient. This troubled me and felt somehow out of alignment.

I loved God and *wanted* to follow any teachings, nudges, and inspirations I believed were *from* God. On my morning jogs near my

Redwood City apartment that week, I'd been deeply contemplating this question and asking God for answers.

A week later, I was completely floored when I read this passage about obedience in *Conversations with God, Book 1*: "Obedience is not creation and thus can never produce salvation. Obedience is a response, while creation is pure choice, undictated, unrequired. Pure choice produces salvation through the pure creation of the highest idea in this moment now."

I was holding a book in my hands that affirmed exactly what I'd been feeling. God was answering my question in a most magical way.

One of the ideas in *Conversations with God* that piqued my interest was the concept of God being *nondual*. This means that everything in our magnificently diverse universe is made in the image of God, not just humans. If I accepted a nondual God, then the whole concept of the Devil, which I'd grown up with, no longer made sense.

We are born with free will, of course, allowing us to engage in evil pursuits if we choose—note that "evil" is "live" spelled backwards—but this is something different than a dual universe with God and the Devil acting in opposition to each other.

Coming to these deeply resonant realizations all at once effectively turned my life upside down—or more accurately, right side up. I felt as though I'd been given the secrets of the universe. I suddenly knew the answers to questions like: Who am I? Why am I here? What can I possibly achieve in life? Who am I in relationship to the rest of humanity and to the Earth?

With these realizations also came the revelation that pursuing my current version of personal success was a child's game compared to what was important to me now. At the end of my life, my career would be meaningless—something I'd done to fill time. What would it mean if I continued to pursue financial success at the expense of close relationships, which were sometimes forced to run on fumes while I was so busy?

What would it mean to have a bank account way beyond anything I could spend in a lifetime, when the accumulating of that bank account would draw precious time away from important work I might do? I wanted to support and nurture others on the conscious journey. People were in pain and in need. Earth's ecosystems also called for my attention.

It became clear that the primary pursuit of my life moving forward would be to evolve and grow into my highest self. My quest would be to become more aware, more responsible, and more mature, and then express these qualities in everything I say and do—both in my interactions with others and with every other aspect of the world.

I began to imagine what life on our planet would be like if everyone on Earth understood that we are all offspring of the Divine. I imagined how different children would be if they were raised in an environment where they were supported to keep those deeper connections we are all surely born with. I imagined what friendships and romantic relationships would be like. I imagined how everyone would naturally care for each other through any and every difficulty. I imagined how differently people would treat animals and the Earth itself.

I came to think of this deeper understanding and the experience of Oneness as the "first domino." If all of humanity could experience it, all the other dominos might fall, so to speak. This would lead to drastic improvements in every aspect of human society—from the way we do business to the way healthcare is delivered. We'd see changes in education, how disagreements are tackled, and the way we make every decision.

I knew this was the path I wanted to pursue. My plan was to try to live these new understandings to the best of my ability.

Stephanie continued to be supportive of the changes that were occurring within me, and the deeper I went into this new understanding of life and the world, the more compelled I felt to focus my energy in this direction. It was clear that simply going around delivering the message would not be effective.

Slowly but surely, my priority became less about top and bottom-line growth for the sake of growth, and more about seeing and serving the sacred in others.

Expansion was still something positive, but not for its own sake. Instead, I became drawn to beneficial enlargement that served and honored my family, the community, and the wider world. The basis for this was spiritual, but I sensed that those around me were not as interested in the spiritual context.

I had come to a "Y" in my path. I could go left and focus on secular advancement or go right and honor spiritual progress. I chose the latter path and pursued my deeper, spiritual journey.

*Conversations with God* had touched something deep within me. I wanted more. This journey felt somewhat isolating, because my colleagues and friends could not relate to the spiritual sensations that resonated with me. The people around me showed that they obviously still cared about me and appreciated me for the person I was. But they couldn't relate to my embrace of spirituality. I felt I was growing in a different direction from those I'd been close to for years, and in some cases, decades.

It seemed to me that if spirituality was to have real meaning, it needed to introduce a more thoughtful and compassionate way of living. My focus was on this. I hoped I might become a more mature and loving person, specifically in my relationships with family, friends, and colleagues.

## 15
# EMBRACING A SUBLIME TRUTH

In Neale's book, I found the God I'd always known—a loving presence, always guiding, always supporting. This God was easy to love. By the time I finished reading the book, I knew I had a huge decision to make. I had to decide if I believed the book's message was true.

If it *was* true, there was no question that I needed to accept its wisdom and, to the best of my ability, embody it in all parts of my life. If I believed the message was false, I could simply set the book on a shelf and forget about it.

I remember sitting with this question, thinking about it, and talking to Stephanie about it. I prayed and meditated, listening carefully for anything God might share with me. I also decided to research various ancient, spiritual texts, to see if there was any support there for the ideas about the nature of God and the human experience Neale described in *Conversations with God*.

What I discovered was that references to the idea of *oneness* and some of the other important truths in the book were to be found everywhere I looked: in the Bible, the Torah, the Qur'an, the Vedas, the Tao Te Ching, the Upanishads, the Bhagavad Gita, and the Buddhist sutras.

This is from the Bible in Acts 17:28: "For in Him we live, move and have our being. As some of your poets have said, 'We are His offspring.'" And, in Ephesians 4:4: "There is one body and one Spirit, just as you were called to one hope when you were called."

Finally, there is the Lord's prayer, which begins: "Our Father, who art in heaven, hallowed be Thy name." But we don't always live our lives as though we truly have a father in heaven; people seem to reserve this realization for Sunday and then it's all but forgotten during the week.

In the lineage of the Catholic Church, the foundation of Jesuit spirituality is that "God is present everywhere and can be found in all creation." The current pontiff, Francis, is the first Jesuit Pope, and here's what he has said:

"We human beings are not only the beneficiaries but also the stewards of other creatures. Thanks to our bodies, God has joined us so closely to the world around us that we can feel the desertification of the soil as a physical ailment, and the extinction of a species as a painful disfigurement. Let us not leave in our wake a swath of destruction and death which will affect our own lives and those of future generations. Nature cannot be seen as something separate from humanity or merely the place we live."

Then there's this from Plato: "Human nature was originally One and we were a whole."

From Hippocrates: "There is one common flow, one common breathing, all things are in sympathy."

From Pierre Teilhard de Chardin: "We are one, after all, you and I. Together we suffer, together exist, and forever will recreate each other."

From Ralph Waldo Emerson: "There is one mind common to all individual men...[a] universal mind. The Over-Soul is that unity...within which every man's particular being is contained and made one with all other. Within man is the soul of the whole...the eternal ONE."

From the Gospel of Thomas: "When you make the two one, and when you make the inner as the outer, and the above as below, and when you make the male and the female into a single one, then you shall enter the kingdom."

And finally, this, from Black Elk: "The first peace, which is the most important, is that which comes within the souls of people when they realize their relationship, their oneness with the universe and all its power, and when they realize that at the center of the universe dwells the Great Spirit, and that this center is really everywhere, it is within each of us."

In my research, I also discovered that even renowned physicists affirm much of what is revealed in the *Conversations with God* books:

"When we view ourselves in space and time, our consciousnesses are obviously the separate individuals of a particle-picture, but when we pass beyond space and time, they may perhaps form ingredients of a single continuous stream of life. As it is with light and electricity, so it may be with life; the phenomena may be individuals carrying on separate existences in space and time, while in the deeper reality beyond space and time we may be all members of one body."

—Sir James Jeans, Astrophysicist

"To divide or multiply consciousness is something meaningless. In all the world, there is no kind of framework within which we can find consciousness in the plural; this is simply something we construct because of the spatio-temporal plurality of individuals, but it is a false construction... The category of number, of whole and of parts, are then simply not applicable to it... The overall number of minds is just one... In truth there is only one mind."

—Erwin Schrodinger, 1933 Nobel Prize in Physics

"The notion of a separate organism is clearly an abstraction, as is also its boundary. Underlying all this is unbroken wholeness even though our civilization has developed in such a way as to strongly emphasize the separation into parts."

—David Bohm & Basil Hiley, physicists

It became clear to me during my research and soul-searching that Neale Donald Walsch's *Conversations with God* was the next extension in a long stream of spiritual, philosophical, and scientific voices down through history, all speaking about the real and foundational significance of our Oneness.

Finally, between my research and my meditations, I had come to the deep clarity that the messages of *Conversations with God* were unequivocally true, which inspired me to live those messages fully from that time forward—not just in my personal or private experiences in my home life, but also in my role as the CEO of ENS.

In your own life, you may, through one means or another, come to epiphanies about the nature and purpose of your life and of Life as a whole. I encourage you to trust those realizations when they arise. They might stand in stark contrast to your normal way of doing things. They may not be the path of least resistance.

A life of deep impact and fulfillment is possible for you. Learning to trust your inner-guidance system is a critical part of finding this destiny.

# 16
# SHIFTING MY LEADERSHIP STYLE

Over the months that followed, I put more effort into expressing the truths I'd discovered in every aspect of my life. I realized I needed to change my leadership style at ENS.

I'd been in the habit of putting "sticky" notes on people's computers over the weekend, to call attention to urgent things that needed to be done. I'm embarrassed to admit this now, but it is true. My notes would greet them as they showed up. They'd be the first thing they saw on Monday morning.

This definitely had to stop; I never wanted to risk any employee feeling they were being diminished or talked down to with a "sticky" message.

I'd also been a big proponent of time management systems. I had scripted everything out before my week began so I could directly manage the things that needed to get done. I now realized my time management style was putting me in a mindset of delegating work to my team, instead of working with them. I needed to throw out my day planner, because it left no space for real, two-way communication with deep listening from the heart. There was nothing sacred in this way of leading and managing.

Since I'd relied on that way of organizing my work life for more than a decade, I was a little bit afraid. Would I destroy ENS when I threw the day-planner out? I wasn't sure an open, flexible, unscripted process could work. Nonetheless, I knew I needed to try. The only way I could look myself in the mirror each day was to live in harmony with my new understandings. That included being true to myself and work with people one-on-one, in the spirit of unity, in a more listening, caring, and spontaneous way.

The day-planner went into the trash.

The team quickly recognized this change. Some even asked if I'd made a conscious choice to become a "more spiritual CEO." I had to explain exactly where I was coming from and all the things I would be managing differently. I also shared with them what I'd been reading, and while it was clear that they weren't interested in joining me on a journey of deep, spiritual awakening at that time in their lives, they seemed to recognize that my ideas might move our business culture in a positive direction.

During my daily lunch hour, I began teaching a course on *Seven Habits of Highly Effective People,* based on the runaway bestseller by Stephen Covey. The Seven Habits are:

1.  Be proactive.

2. Begin with the end in mind.

3. Put first things first.

4. Think win-win.

5. Seek first to understand, then to be understood.

6. Synergize.

7. Sharpen the saw (which means, find ways to renew your physical, social/emotional, mental, and spiritual areas).

Through what I taught in the *Seven Habits* training, I found a way to deliberately instill spiritual principles into the process of selling, supporting, and leading our business. There were no shortcuts or "win/lose" strategies. My strategy would be about everyone winning. I developed a heart-based, long-term approach to conducting business.

The training also emphasized spirituality in personal growth. In addition to listing spirituality as one of the four dimensions of life we all needed to "sharpen," it also stressed that the spirit of win-win could not survive in an environment of competition. I fully embraced these concepts, and I found teaching the program fulfilling.

Stephen Covey was a deeply spiritual person. One of his desk calendars said: "Achieving Unity—Oneness—with ourselves, with our friends and working associates, is the highest and best and most delicious fruit of the Seven Habits." When combined with "Identity is destiny," that message is particularly powerful.

After making this shift in my business life, I was initially shocked to discover that ENS was growing even more rapidly than before. But it made sense. How could a company *not* become more effective when leadership moves into a place of more open, loving, and listening interactions?

Employees and customers alike seemed thrilled. Our vendors almost couldn't believe it, as they were accustomed to being at the bottom of the food chain. To be treated with a new level of dignity and respect was surprising and even a little confusing for them.

With my shift into this more conscious way of operating, everyone the business touched felt cared about, and that led to referral after referral. Our spiritual way of doing business contributed to the company's high-speed expansion.

In your own life, I encourage you to experiment with living more intentionally in this same way. Make love your foundation and see if the universe doesn't respond by delivering positive experiences right to your door.

## 17
# BECOMING MORE CONSCIOUS

All my life, I'd felt close to a God who guided and supported me. My spirituality came from my own experiences, not from a religion.

In my early years, my family attended a Catholic church weekly. At one point, I even briefly served as an altar boy at Sunday mass —but the parish priest was not forgiving when I poured too much water or wine into his cup during the service. He also sometimes asked me to donate the tips I received following wedding ceremonies.

The church felt steeped in tradition, but I didn't feel much *love* there, which was in sharp contrast to the God I'd grown close to. That was a God who was unconditionally loving, guiding me to more mature decisions as I grew up in a single-parent household. That God provided me with opportunities to be the best person I could be.

I had sensed God in nature as a boy in my forested backyard, when I chased leaves as they cascaded from tall trees. I'd felt that God protected me when I rode in cars and on motorcycles with friends who drove recklessly, although I now see it was a miracle we managed to stay on the road. I'd even felt God's hand on my shoulder when, at twenty-two, I followed my soul's calling and made that big move from my home near Washington, D.C. to San Francisco, where I had few connections and was very much on my own.

I'd always felt God was there for me when I needed help or guidance. He/She wasn't a judgmental or frightening presence. I felt a nurturing, forgiving God—a God who loved me.

Through Neale Donald Walsch's *Conversations with God: Book 1*, I felt called to a different kind of connection to God, something more than personal trust and guidance. God wanted me to become fully awake, conscious, and aware of the deeper truth that I am a spiritual being inhabiting a physical body, while also being part of something bigger. My new goal was to see myself as an individuation of the Divine, a wondrous expression of life, and a willing steward of the Earth.

I had come to Silicon Valley in 1979 to pursue my dreams of well-being and success. Businesses were creating great financial wealth there, and they continue to do so. Within fifteen years, I was well on my way to achieving my own great wealth.

But in 1995, as I was awakening to new understandings about life and becoming more conscious, the race to success felt Newtonian, where the visible and invisible worlds were separate. In Silicon Valley, in that era, the social Darwinist treasure was something to be endlessly gathered and stored. Life there was about survival of the fittest.

Suddenly, this no longer felt like a meaningful way to live in the world. I was sure that one person could make a difference, and that it was a matter of *will*, not potential or capacity. I believe everyone can make a mighty contribution.

The question is: "Will we?"

As I continued to research the messages of *Conversations with God*, I did my best to embody their wisdom. As I've mentioned, I read the Bible and sacred texts from a variety of faith traditions. I filled my bookshelf with spiritual texts from contemporary authors such as Kahlil Gibran, Gerald Jampolsky, Wayne Dyer, Deepak Chopra, Bruce H. Lipton, Marianne Williamson, Dean Radin, Paul Ferrini, Ken Wilber, and others.

In the summer of 1995, and the months that followed, I experimented with ways my life could express the wisdom I discovered in these writings. My deeper spiritual journey had officially begun.

## 18
# NEW BEGINNINGS AND MAGICAL MOMENTS

At this point, I'd like to set aside my at-the-office career and share a little more about my home life. I'm doing so for a specific reason that involves the overall intention of this book.

When people consider the larger purpose of life, they might assume that the wonderful details of their private lives are unimportant. I have learned that quite the opposite is true.

I've come to see that the private and personal pieces of life's puzzle can be an extraordinarily meaningful element of the bigger picture. For someone who strives to make a positive difference in the world, these details can be more important than we might first imagine.

One of the most significant personal encounters of my own life can serve as an example of how a private experience led me to choices that later directly affected the world at large.

By this time in my journey (the mid-'90s), Stephanie and I had been dating and growing closer for almost four years. She was supportive of the spiritual growth that was transforming my life and pointing me in a new direction. As I felt my passion shift from entrepreneurial activity to my spiritual life, she made it clear she was behind me completely.

After all the time we'd spent together, I was sure Stephanie was the one for me and that God had brought us together. I decided I'd ask her to marry me during a picturesque hike at Julia Pfeiffer Burns State Park in Big Sur. I wanted it to be a surprise, but without thinking, I had stuffed the engagement ring in its large box into my fanny pack, where it created an obvious and unusual bulge that immediately caught Stephanie's attention.

As we were heading out the door for the hike, she pointed at my pack and said, "What's that?"

I playfully swatted her hand away and told her it was nothing, hoping she wouldn't think twice about it. That didn't work. During the entire hike, she seemed jumpy and scared. I was almost afraid to follow through with my plan. Fortunately, once we'd reached a perfect spot on the trail, I worked up my courage, went down on one knee, and popped the question.

She said yes! It was another unforgettable, magical moment.

These small but important parts of life often bring us long-lasting, life-enriching outcomes. I decided to never again hold back on an idea that lit up my heart and soul. I'll share more of these life-altering and people-impacting ideas in the chapters ahead—but first, this chapter of my story isn't quite complete.

Once Stephanie and I were engaged, we quickly began discussing how and where we'd get married. I initially championed a large ceremony with all our friends and family, but my fiancé liked the idea of a small, destination wedding with just the two of us. Her parents were divorced, as were mine; I had to agree that we didn't need to add family politics to our celebration.

Stephanie learned that the United States honored wedding ceremonies that took place in Fiji, but not in other tropical locations such as Tahiti. We chose the Fijian island of Wakaya. It's a breathtaking location and a regular destination for exotic honeymoons, but few weddings—at least at that time.

The ceremony was set for October 16, 1997 on the beach. Some of the local islanders took part in the ceremony; others gathered nearby to celebrate with us. We decided that, instead of walking down the aisle, Stephanie would ride on a wooden raft, rowed by a couple of the Fijian men, down to where I waited in front of our wood-and-thatch *bure*—a Fijian hut built from wood and straw.

Unfortunately, as she started this short trip, a sudden wind came up and began to push the raft further out to sea. I could feel my anxiety start to rise. Thankfully, her escorts were strong enough to wrestle the wayward raft back to the intended landing site, where Stephanie and I took our vows. Stephanie was a beautiful bride. I felt so blessed to have met her and to be able to marry her in such a magical place.

Looking back later on our engagement and wedding, I saw that both days delivered a message: Never assume, when things get slightly out of sync, that you won't arrive at the intended destination. I've made it a point to remember that it doesn't serve me to embrace a worst-case scenario just because things don't go the way I think they should.

This is especially important when you consider the complicated matter of shifting your life's purpose.

Once Stephanie and I were back in California, it was obvious to me that our two-week vacation from the office had been medicine for my soul, and I knew she felt the same way. We returned to work as a happily married couple, feeling renewed and ready to get back to work.

# 19
# TRANSPARENCY AND PIVOTING
# IN NEW DIRECTIONS

I became intrigued with Open-Book Management (OBM), an innovation pioneered by Jack Stack, founder of the SRC Holding Corporation. The strategy involves training a company's entire staff to read financial statements; creating a process to review the statements with the whole team on a regular basis; developing shared goals; and then giving bonuses to share the wealth when the team met those goals.

This approach involves extreme transparency. The entire team shares all information, and they are rewarded based on results. I could only imagine the trust and teamwork this would generate. Bringing the whole company together to review financial results—with a focus on producing more revenue with less waste and higher profit levels—would also give us an opportunity to discuss other important matters. I set to work adopting Open-Book Management at our company.

We began to meet monthly to review our financial statements and check out our position compared to the metrics we'd set. The company's growth again soared.

Meanwhile, the networking industry continued to explode. Our ENS engineers gained valuable experience honing their skills across both campus and global network environments; as they became more knowledgeable, we began to offer consulting practices focused on fine-tuning application and network performance. We realized we were pushing into new technical areas when Cisco Systems tapped us to educate other industry partners.

In the early 1990s, there were still people who thought the Internet wouldn't last. Maybe it was just a fad. But in fact, the personal computer revolution was just getting started. Each year, people were spending more time sitting in front of computers, surfing the Web to connect with news, email, and social media. In-house-only, "local" PC applications were becoming less important.

Most companies were struggling to keep up with this exponential increase in computer use. Because networking is deeply technical, most engineers had to scale a series of steep learning curves to understand newer technologies. ENS was at the leading edge of each new curve. We were in a strong position to help heal the growing pains and navigate the complexities for these companies.

Our "application performance" practice opened new frontiers in consulting services, even as our integration practice was skyrocketing. New, more specialized consulting practices were beginning to open. We were flying high.

During this time, I read a classic book for entrepreneurs and business people called *Crossing the Chasm*. Author Geoffrey Moore focused on the reality that hardware profit margins will always erode over time. This is true of every form of hardware on every level, from tiny computer chips to office computers to complex communications platforms, such as those that served as the center of our customer-communication hubs.

Erosion had deep implications for our business, because the value of hardware was a substantial part in our profit mix. I could see that, within the next couple of years, our industry would undergo enormous change. The future clearly belonged to organizations that did not rely on profits from hardware as a big part of their revenue.

I was working closely at that time with Noel Fenton, chairman of Trinity Ventures. He encouraged me to name an organization that might be the future for ENS customers and personnel. After reviewing candidates, I settled on the NEC Business Communications Group, a Japanese conglomerate.

NEC was a leader in voice communication systems and they were interested in expanding into voice, data, and video integration. We were a perfect fit for their expansion plans because we were a leader in these areas. On December 31, 1997, we announced NEC's $5 million investment in ENS with a convertible option to sell the integration segment of our business, but not the consulting segment, which would remain as an independent entity.

This meant our staff could find a long-term home at ENS, without concern for eroding hardware margins, recessions that come and go, and financial investment to carry it for the long term.

Meanwhile, all sectors of the business world were undergoing revolutionary change. The Internet was turning whole industries on their heads. Everything that happened online seemed to move at the speed of light: communications, order flow, supply chains, and delivery of products to customers.

The Internet enabled a total shift in business communications. Across the industry, data, voice, and video applications were migrating to this new medium, and web-savvy start-up organizations began to challenge traditional business models.

To remain competitive, companies needed to leverage network and application technologies to defend and grow core businesses—but this was a daunting task, which created the new consulting business opportunity.

As we moved into the mid to late 1990s, these consulting services were out on the edge and in high demand, so Rich and I decided to launch a new company based on consulting.

# 20
# THE MEANING OF TRUE WEALTH

I set up a meeting with John Chambers, the CEO of Cisco Systems, to discuss the consulting business opportunity. We'd seen each other several times since the early '90s when he came to our South San Francisco ENS office to discuss our partnering with Cisco. This was only the second time we'd planned to meet one-on-one.

Because we both had such busy schedules, the only time we could meet in John's San Jose office happened to be on the day of Stephanie's thirtieth birthday. My best intentions aside, the day did not start out well. Thirty is obviously a milestone birthday, so I should have planned a thoughtful beginning to her day. Unfortunately, I had not given this much thought. Although I had a nice dinner and gifts planned for later, for breakfast, I just grabbed stale muffins from the refrigerator and stuck candles in them.

The look on Stephanie's face was a terrible mixture of sadness and disappointment. I felt awful for failing her in the first morning moments of her birthday. I apologized profusely, promising to do a better job with future festivities. I knew I never wanted to disappoint *myself* in that way again, by being or giving less than I know I can be and give.

This was another of those small events in my private life that were powerfully significant. I could have easily "written off" my failure at the time as being just a product of my upbringing. As I've mentioned, I'd grown up in a home with a single mother and six brothers and sisters;

we were accustomed to throwing such things together at the last minute without any fanfare. But Stephanie had grown up in a home with only one sister, so birthdays were a big deal.

I knew there was something for me to glean from this experience, and I've recounted it here so that you, too, can benefit. My lesson was about paying attention to the so-called "little things" in life, such as small choices and actions, and noticing the feelings that follow. This is how we gather all the emotional information we need to make major decisions, including those about people we love.

I'm glad that moment in the kitchen on Stephanie's thirtieth birthday stuck with me. It has helped guide me in making huge decisions, precisely *because* I was determined never to disappoint myself again.

One huge decision came later, after my meeting with John. I had shared my plans to spin off the consulting and professional services business from ENS and set it up as an independent company. I asked John outright if he'd like to invest in that venture. While I hadn't put together a business plan or prospectus yet, we were looking to raise $7.5 million in an "A" round of financing.

Even without a business plan, John said he felt this was a reasonable offer. We shook hands and I met with his mergers and acquisition guy to work out the details. A few months later, the new company, which we later named Netigy, was almost ready to roll. We would have a nucleus of fifty staff members in place for the launch.

Once our deal was approved, I felt I could relax, with that funding secured.

Meanwhile, my spiritual evolution was continuing. I often silently recited something I heard from spiritual teachers: *We have a spiritual basis; this is our true identity, but it needs to be nurtured for the light within to become activated.*

I had become accustomed to attending upscale business retreats at swank resorts in luxurious locations. Now these expensive events triggered a cognitive dissonance in me. Both the time and the money I was spending in this way didn't feel congruent with my deeper purpose in life, especially when there were so many people dealing with daily hardship.

I was acutely aware that many people—and the Earth itself—were severely challenged. During a private moment, I shared this with Stephanie. I was not surprised when she told me she'd been sensing the same thing.

Some of the ideas I'd brought home from those retreats were valuable, but I had to question how much more of our resources I wanted to spend this way.

At one of the most valuable of those programs, a Harvard University lecturer had asked us to define "the meaning of true wealth." He suggested prioritizing our family culture and family values instead of financial wealth. The standard to which we hold ourselves in our families is our *true* wealth.

I couldn't help but see the contradiction between this idea and what I'd thought it meant to be "successful" in today's world. The way we grow up and our life experiences give us an inner image of what success looks like. This image can be the prime mover of our decision-making, often unconsciously setting us on a course to what we imagine to be our destiny.

But if the image is influenced by the culture in which you live, it can create a mythology that does one of two things: it either inspires you to be the best you can be, or it works like a poison in your life and the lives of everyone around you, stealing joy and causing harm.

In the West, that success mythology centers around money, power, and fame. People judge their value based on their ability to be successful in those three areas. What about qualities like honesty, generosity, and spirituality? Those traits are seen as having *some* value, but they're not considered necessary ingredients for success. Indeed, they are often perceived as liabilities.

The mainstream definition of success obviously didn't align with what the Harvard lecturer shared, and I realized it didn't align with my own later definition of success, either. It was clear to me that the entire culture needed to shift away from this false and unfulfilling definition.

Chasing money, power, and fame is a major cause of the massive individual and collective dysfunction that dominates modern society.

We had a lot of work to do.

# 21
# SHIFTING TO A NEW AND GRANDER PURPOSE

Despite our rapid growth at ENS, the sailing wasn't always smooth. We faced our share of challenges and headaches.

A cardinal rule in business is to cultivate several sources of income. If a single customer makes up a large percentage of your total revenue, it can put your business in a perilous situation. Two of our largest San Francisco Bay Area customers let us know, at around the same time, that they were exploring other options for their supplies and services. If we lost both accounts, we'd have had to lay off 25 percent of our staff.

I had ideas for how we could save these customers, and I felt sure we could save at least one if we sprang into action.

Working with our account teams, we made a few adjustments to beef up our resources; these moves ultimately convinced both accounts to remain with ENS. This close call had everyone's nerves on edge, but we worked it out—for the time being.

Open-book management smoothed the way as we prepared to sell the network integration segment of our business to NEC. Our leadership team had become self-managing; with each passing month, Rich and I were able to be less involved in the company's day-to-day operations and even strategic discussions.

In late 1998, the national and global economy were both robust. Investment in network infrastructure was still growing exponentially. It felt like the ideal time to transfer our network integration division to NEC and to launch what was to become Netigy.

As you can imagine, I gained a great deal of satisfaction from having created ENS, and not simply because of the money we made on the sale of the company. I learned so much that I took with me about working with others in high-powered endeavors. These lessons proved wonderfully beneficial when I shifted my life toward a new and grander purpose.

We had set out to build a great company, and we had done it! ENS became known as an integrator that was about much more than just selling and supporting data communications products. Our culture was activist, even before this was common in Silicon Valley. We attracted and retained the best people, largely because of our in-house practices.

Our team members understood our strong stakeholder orientation and they were grateful for our transparency. Our staff also appreciated our advocacy for the communities surrounding our office locations.

In the final month, Rich and I decided to give 20 percent of the sale price to the employees who had helped us build the integration division.

## 22
# THE BEGINNING OF THE END

**N**ot long after the ENS sale, one of Silicon Valley's top venture capital companies told us they might be interested in partnering through investment. They were eager to fund a new network services start-up, but they wanted to focus on the service provider segment of the market—not the enterprise market, where Netigy had primarily been focusing.

Service providers were consultancies and companies that remotely managed a customer's IT infrastructure. Within that sector, jobs were more specialized. On the enterprise side, network engineers had to be "jack-of-all-trades" with mastery over a broader array of skills.

The proposed deal also called for a commitment from me to remain as CEO, at least during the few years of the company's formative stages.

While this company's offer was attractive, we'd been extraordinarily successful by focusing on enterprise accounts. Would it be wise to change strategies now? I worried about our ability to align and quickly scale if we made the leap to this other industry segment.

The Enterprise Networking experience had exhausted me. I'd given myself fully to the growth and scaling of ENS, and I wasn't sure I wanted to commit to becoming CEO of Netigy. I believed a better position for me would be Executive Chairman. In that role, I could coach and guide the new CEO and take part in operational meetings, but the CEO would carry the day-to-day responsibility for the operations and setting the stage to enable the company to grow.

For these reasons, I decided to explore the idea of partnering with two other venture capital companies, rather than the firm that had approached us. The executive of one of these firms said he was confident we could connect with strong CEO candidates. He even offered to begin a search immediately upon inking a deal.

That did it for me. I made the decision to go with this other firm and notified all the parties involved. The investor that had first contacted me was not happy about my decision; in less than a year, they decided to fund another company, which would become our competitor in the market. My choice might have been a strategic error, as it quickly created more direct competition for us.

Our CEO search went into high gear as soon as I decided on our venture partners. We set up brief interviews with candidates who were leading technology or services organizations. I later recognized that our approach to this was also flawed.

I met these candidates briefly over lunch, in an airport, or in a confidential office somewhere. I would make a quick assessment and then try to bring the person on board, if they looked like a fit. I had no way to completely understand someone, or their way of collaborating with a team, under such rushed circumstances.

To add to the challenge, I didn't yet understand the true value of hiring people whose vision and values were more closely aligned with my own. I was recruiting and considering candidates without paying enough attention to their core values.

I think we were more effective in looking for the Netigy executive team that would report to the CEO and president. We developed a recruiting process that found and quickly landed top talent. We recruited them from industry leaders and from top services organizations.

We wound up with an extraordinary group of seasoned professionals, bright and hardworking. Most of them had managed teams much larger than those they would be asked initially to manage at Netigy. I was glad to have them aboard as we moved forward. We found and hired a CEO, and we continued to grow.

Following the ENS sale in May, 1999, Netigy had about fifty employees. A year and a half later, in July of 2000, we were nearing 650 employees working from more than thirty offices in the U.S. and overseas. We had a London office, and other European locations were opening shortly. We made plans to expand to Asia and Australia.

To fund this growth, we raised $104 million in our "B" round of financing. Rich and I decided to invest $2 million each, a large chunk of our after-tax sale amount from ENS. I saw this investment as my way of participating financially in Netigy's growth prospects.

I had placed my Netigy stock in a Farrell Family Charitable Trust, which Stephanie and I created to support the philanthropic activity we were planning.

We raised $75 million in our "C" round of financing. At this point, Netigy was carrying a post-money valuation of more than $600 million.

All looked well. All seemed well. All was not well.

# 23
# TROUBLE IN PARADISE

I think our problem from the beginning was a major error in focus. During the Netigy launch celebration, our company's president took the stage. I should have known we were in deep trouble when, during his remarks, he said: "It's about the money, stupid."

All our success over the years had been the result of focusing on building a great company. For me, for Stephanie, and for Rich, it was *never* just about the money. Now, as we were intending to inspire members of our team, the focus was turning to *just* making money.

I was truly upset with this turn of events. When I reached out to board members to share my thoughts, they ignored my concerns.

During this same period, a company called International Network Services called me to see if we'd be willing to sell Netigy at a substantial valuation. But because our ventures had never been primarily about the money, I turned them down. I wasn't interested in selling out just as we were getting started.

When I told our CEO and Board of Directors about my decision later, they were upset that I hadn't consulted them first.

Should we have sold Netigy at once, "getting out while the getting was good?" It didn't feel like the right move at the time, and it doesn't feel that way now. But the truth is, I never *did* consult with our Board or the CEO about the offer, so I must take full responsibility for this decision. I was also responsible for the disharmony this created.

Then things became more difficult. Rich let me know that while he still desired to keep his co-ownership of Netigy, he wanted to step away from the company's day-to-day workings. He had never been an advocate of building out the new professional services organization, and he was not happy, so I didn't try to persuade him to stay.

I could not have known at the time that Rich's absence would make things far more challenging for Netigy.

I knew we needed a strong chief technology officer to assure a smooth transition from the pioneering work we'd done to boost network performance to the new consulting products we envisioned. I didn't realize that without Rich, this transition would turn out to be anything but smooth. Our core competency became diluted by all the new faces, who understood little about the network services space.

Those within the new company didn't have a great deal of enthusiasm for the role I had chosen to play. I, too, had stepped out of day-to-day operations—but I had wanted to be Executive Chairman so I could guide the team and help with our strategic planning and partnerships. After a while, it became clear that the executives I'd hired to replace me saw things differently.

The board members seemed to think of me as someone on the outside who had no vital role. One member of the executive team accused me of being a "seagull manager"—someone who swoops in, makes noise, and poops all over everything.

In one executive meeting, the first person to speak then called on someone else to contribute to the conversation, and then that person called on someone else, and so on. They called on me last. I could sense they did this deliberately.

I'd been in the lead for the first ten years of ENS and Netigy, but now I could see that I was considered unnecessary—or worse. It was a troubling time. I began to realize that I was a chairman in title only, not in function.

Things began to deteriorate about the time we closed our "C" round of financing in the fall of 2000. Technology companies had come under pressure when their stocks began to fall, back in the spring of that year, and had begun to rein in their infrastructure budgets.

I knew we needed to become more focused, lay off staff, and go into cash-conservation mode. But this did not happen.

About this time, our CEO came to me to ask if he should turn his attention to selling the company. I thought this was a horrible idea.

"Who would want to buy us when we are burning so much cash?" I asked. "We can focus on adjusting the company by identifying our most promising application areas and reducing staff, or we can focus on selling something—assuming we have something saleable— but we can't do both things at once."

Everything was on the line. I called board members to share that we seemed to have lost our way and were in danger of losing the company, but it was to no avail.

On September 10, 2001, we signed papers to sell Netigy's assets and transition most of our employees to a company called Thrupoint, based in New York.

Netigy had attracted the best and brightest employees in the data communications industry. Our early team leaders were drawn to a vision of building a great company. We were not able to manifest that vision—but our sales, engineering, technical, marketing, finance, and legal leadership were truly off the charts. I was grateful to work with so many talented people during the early days of this endeavor, and I am happy that the sale of strategic assets to Thrupoint permitted the majority of our employees to keep their jobs.

As cofounder and chairman of Netigy, I had been responsible for recruiting the first investors and the CEO. I therefore bear much of the responsibility for the loss of so much investor capital, including Rich's and my own. While I am certainly sorry for that, I've also come to see that there is great truth to the adage: "When one door closes, another one opens."

For me, the Netigy experience was exactly that. With the company sold, it was finally possible for me to begin to move toward my life's great passion, a journey that had been years in the making.

# 24
# THE 'SUGAR HIGH' OF WEALTH PURSUIT

In the two years following the sale of ENS, my financial wealth had ballooned, but something continued to not feel right. I had pursued my dreams and I was now tasting the rewards in a substantial way—but life was not what I'd expected. I never had a pinnacle, "I'm there!" experience. And because our second start-up, Netigy, didn't work out as planned, I never found a pinnacle there, either.

I was concerned about the level of dysfunction in the world and the direction humanity was headed. I saw wealth creation all around me, but it looked like the pursuit of financial wealth was an unquenchable thirst. Those who had $500 million were setting their sights on $1 billion in net worth, and that goal would double again when they achieved it. Those with a four-person jet wanted one that would seat eight.

I realized that, in the world of wealth pursuit, nobody reached a sense of feeling "full." Any inclination toward supporting charitable causes in a substantial way would often be postponed, to rationalize making more money. A friend of a friend, who had a $925 million net worth, said he planned to contribute to charities, but not until he was worth a billion!

In most cases, financial net worth just continues to grow. People wanted to compare even more favorably to others with great financial wealth. And while many with extreme wealth have signed the 50 percent or more "giving pledge" created by Bill Gates and Warren Buffet, in most cases, financial wealth continues to balloon exponentially, year after year, for the top 1 percent.

At the same time, almost everyone else seems to have less and less.

This is because financial wealth is grown and harvested through equity investment, which allows the rich to become richer and the poor to become poorer. The planet with immediate needs gets little focus, even though a sizable portion of the people living here desperately need resources and the Earth's ecosystems desperately need attention.

Good jobs require professional training; those without training languish in low-skill, low-paying employment.

When a business is *conscious*, the owners understand clearly that all of life is deeply interconnected. Life becomes the paramount consideration. The business collaborates to design products and services that support and enhance the lives of people, the planet, and all of life inhabiting the planet.

Of course, as with any business, there must be a "unique value proposition"—a need going unfulfilled that the business will address. Revenue and profit growth follow. The business creates prosperity for itself and the surrounding community.

When a business ignores the interconnectedness of life and acts in a reductive and analytical way, it skips all the initial steps and goes straight to finding something that people are willing to pay for. If there is a market for an oil extraction system that blasts carbon emissions into the atmosphere, a GMO for agriculture, or a media company that is popular but deceiving, the business moves rapidly ahead to production. The focus is on maximizing revenue and profits. This process can and often does overlook the trade-offs they make. They trade soul satisfaction for earthly treasure.

To me, this way of doing business feels like a process where we trade off real intrinsic value for a financially created alternate reality. People believe they can find security and satisfaction simply through financial net worth. I believe this creates a kind of "sugar high," and just like the rush of eating a high-carb treat, when it wears off, we feel worse.

I've repeatedly seen that when investors must choose between real, intrinsic value and financial success, they almost always choose the money. Our current culture considers financial wealth the be-all and end-all. This has placed enormous pressure on businesses to deliver stellar quarter-over-quarter results, no matter the cost.

Financial prosperity is a wonderful tool for nurturing families, communities, and the world around us. But when the goal is to fund multiple estates, private jets, and other measures of financial success—or when the wealth sits idle in a bank account so the owner can feel he is richer than other wealthy people—then prosperity is a cancer.

I was right smack in the middle of this success paradigm when it became clear to me that I was being called to something else.

It might seem hard to believe, but just as life is painful for those who have too little money to pay for their life expenses, it also can be painful for those stuck gathering more and more financial treasure with no sense of "full." On the outside—and especially to those who hold fast to chasing the "success" dream—wealthy people look like they "have it all." They look like compelling examples of success. But on the inside, they feel unfulfilled.

They are stuck in a race where there's no "there" there. They focus on the ladder of financial success and compare themselves to those above them on the ladder. They often are tired and fatigued. Their close relationships often suffer from lack of attention. They pay little regard to the small voice within them; their inner callings go mostly unheeded. The outer appearance of success masks the crises just below the surface.

Many "successful" people live with a sense of unspoken, quiet desperation. They have traded off time with their spouse or their children, who often encounter a host of problems as they're growing up, and close friends who feel abandoned and then become increasingly unavailable.

They keep these aspects of their lives out of public view and might even feel a sense of shame about these personal failures.

I saw this firsthand when I lived in Silicon Valley. Extremely wealthy people can become depressed and even suicidal.

I know this may sound odd or out of place, but I believe that everyone in pain deserves our help. We might hold close those who suffer from financial poverty, but it's easy to dismiss the pain of those who suffer from extreme wealth, fame, and fortune.

We are all One. None of us can be truly prosperous and free until all of us are prosperous and free.

From time to time, many of us lose our way. Sometimes we carry others on our backs. Sometimes they carry us.

## 25
# CLOSING DOORS SO NEW DOORS CAN OPEN

On the evening of September 10, 2001, Stephanie and I drove to Big Sur, where we had a two-night reservation at the Post Ranch Inn. We walked to a private, undeveloped part of the property and stood on a sheer cliff about 500 feet above the beach.

Overlooking the Pacific, Stephanie and I symbolically tossed sticks and stones over the precipice to the rocky shore below to signify the closing of old doors as new doors were opening. My career as a technology executive was officially finished. I'd learned valuable lessons that I knew I would take with me into the next chapter of my life.

My spiritual journey was about to take a giant leap forward.

In a sense, I was leaving something I was *paid* for, to do what I was *made* for. My new chapter would be about aligning with the Divine and giving my full attention to service work. I had no doubt that my work and my family would be blessed in the process.

The next morning, September 11, 2001, Stephanie and I woke up prepared to enjoy a quiet breakfast. The Post Ranch Inn does not have televisions or newspapers. We enjoyed a buffet at the restaurant, which has a sweeping view of the Pacific, all the way to the distant horizon. Sometimes you can see whales migrating along the coast.

We noticed faxes piling up in the center of the breakfast area. This seemed odd, because this location was all about quiet conversation and contemplation—not written material and news accounts.

I was curious, so I went over and grabbed one of the faxes. It said that the second World Trade Center tower had just "been hit" and had collapsed. Stephanie and I read this in shock. The fax had mentioned the "second tower," so I went back and found an earlier fax that explained how an airplane had crashed into the first tower, hours earlier.

We spent the rest of our morning quietly contemplating what had happened and praying for all those who were injured or killed, along with the countless families who were directly dealing with the horror of the attacks.

The timing of the events that were unfolding felt a little beyond coincidence for me. The previous day, we had signed papers to turn over the assets of Netigy to another company, and my duties as chairman of the board were complete. Moving forward, I was going to live my life in service to conscious evolution and my family.

And there we were, one day later, learning about terrorists who had committed one of the most heinous acts in modern history, killing thousands of people. Among other things, the terrorist attack revealed just how great the need for conscious evolution truly is.

Stephanie and I were especially stunned by the timing, and not just the magnitude of what had happened. The world was changing, less than twenty-four hours after the Netigy sale. I felt as though the Divine had freed me up at this moment to play a new role, perhaps even somehow connected with this tragedy. I was not at all certain what that new role would be.

It would be nearly eighteen months before my next steps became clear. During that year and a half, I was certain that I was to play a role in the planetary awakening process. I used this time to listen to my own soul's calling and to tighten and strengthen my personal relationship with the Divine.

In the weeks and months following my departure from Netigy, I brought closure to other aspects of my life that needed my attention. I spent time reviewing the changes in my life with my closest friends. I shared that my journey was shifting me away from being business-focused and into something more conscious and spiritual.

My gut was telling me that I needed to become actively involved in an emerging spirituality that could contribute to a more conscious humanity. There was no question that I'd completely lost my passion for the Silicon Valley business world.

People began using the term "sustainability" during this time. Most people I was in touch with shared my concerns about the planetary crisis confronting us; they agreed that the Earth might become uninhabitable if we continued burning fossil fuels and releasing carbon dioxide into the atmosphere. They also agreed that social injustice was threatening the lives and quality of life for too much of the planet's population.

But the conversation stopped there. They all thought I was unwise to leave the business world to pursue a spiritual calling.

I could feel their concern for me and appreciated that they were trying to warn me away from the trouble they were sure I'd encounter if I continued trying to point my life in an entirely new direction. Yet I was undaunted. I believed, in my heart, that an emerging spirituality could create the change humanity needed to course-correct away from the perilous future we were careening toward.

What if every child was born into an environment that allowed them to develop a deep understanding that they were, in fact, offspring of the Divine? How might this awareness create new relationships with each other and with the Earth? How might it spawn new forms of business and organization? How much different might the world look if we were all fully aware of our Oneness?

I didn't have the answers to these questions, but I suspected an emerging spirituality could create transformative change—just the kind of wholesale change that was needed to turn the world right side up. Most people I spoke to about this idea thought it was utterly impossible, and when I looked at the issue with my logical mind, I couldn't disagree with them.

But since I felt the truth of these ideas in my bones, I knew I had to set out on this mission, no matter where it led me.

Have you had similar moments that forced you to choose between having faith in your own inner knowing and the perspective of others? Most of us will face this dilemma; when you do, I urge you to trust that intuitive sense if it seems to come from the core of your being—even if a thousand external voices are shouting at you to go a different way.

That inner sense is often the Divine's most direct way of communicating with you and inspiring you to follow its direction. This wisdom will guide you somewhere that is fruitful for your evolving personal journey. It will work every time.

## 26
# MY 'HOW I MET NEALE DONALD WALSCH' STORY

When Neale Donald Walsch's *Conversations with God* hit the book stores in 1995, it made a huge splash. In fact, some journalists described its success as an international phenomenon. *Conversations with God Book 1: An Uncommon Dialogue* stayed on the *New York Times* bestseller list for 137 weeks and has been translated into thirty-seven languages. Its insights and wisdom changed the lives of the millions of readers around the world—including me.

As a result of the book's success, Neale became an overnight celebrity and was invited to be a guest on television programs such as *The Today Show* and *Larry King Live*. He made numerous other national and local public speaking appearances. But even with this attention, there are people who have never heard of him or his book.

I have often wondered why the messages from *Conversations with God*—along with the messages of other similar classical and contemporary books—are not more well-known, understood, and accepted among the population at large. These messages can change lives.

New wisdom, even when supported by science, has historically been targeted and marginalized by the authorities. Only after years of rigorous research and volleys of debate back and forth do new truths emerge to see the light of day.

Just look at what happened to early mathematicians and astronomers who proposed the heliocentric theory (Earth and other planets revolve around the sun) in opposition to the then prevailing geocentric theory (Earth at the center of the universe)!

Nicolaus Copernicus proposed a heliocentric system in works published in 1543. The Catholic Church promptly deemed this research heretical and issued a prohibition against it. Giordano Bruno, an advocate of the Copernican theory, was burned at the stake for his unorthodox views. Then, when Galileo, a physicist and astronomer, surfaced in support of the Copernican theory, he was forced to recant his scientific findings and he spent the rest of his life under house arrest.

In time, these men were exonerated. From the late 16th century onward, the heliocentric model gradually superseded the geocentric model. Copernicus has been called the initiator of a scientific revolution, a complete change in the way the world was viewed.

This might be what is about to occur now: a new scientific revolution. The stars may be aligning for it. The Bible and other sacred texts offer more than enough validation for the idea that all of life is made in the image and likeness of God, the Divine. Another way of saying this is to declare that everything is the offspring of one thing, and that this one thing can be called God, the Divine, the Universe, Life, Love, or something else—but does the name really matter?

In *The Psychology of Religion and Spirituality* (April, 2019), a peer-reviewed online journal, L.M. Edinger-Schons writes in "Oneness Beliefs and Their Effect on Life Satisfaction":

"The idea of oneness can be traced back to ancient philosophy. The Presocratics already discussed 'the one' as the first principle of all being things. The argument of the 'one over the many' (*hen epi pollon*) was introduced by Plato, meaning that the simple 'one' always has to come before the complex 'many.' The Neoplatonist Plotinus (205–270 C.E.) saw the transcendent 'ONE' (τò ν) as the source of all things. In his theory, all embodied individual souls are permanently rooted in this first principle. The idea of all things being rooted in one underlying, unifying principle has persisted from the Presocratics as the first documented western philosophers to modern-day esotericism in the 21st century.

The notion of being at one with a divine principle, life, the world, other people, or even activities has been discussed in various religious traditions, but also in a wide variety of scientific research streams from different disciplines. Thereby, research results from various disciplines point to the positive effects of feeling at one with life, connected to others, or connected to nature on adaptation, well-being, and life satisfaction."

Many contemporary scientists are devoting their lives to this study of "oneness" as a Divine or universal principle. Nassim Haramein, a leader in unified physics, has created a body of work called *The Connected Universe* asserting that everything is part of one field. Dean Radin, PhD, Chief Scientist at the Institute of Noetic Science, also reveals that things are not as separate as they seem; in reality, he asserts, everything is deeply entangled. Bruce H. Lipton, PhD, a cellular biologist and one-time researcher at Stanford, also supports this body of work, and wrote a book with Steve Bhaerman titled *Spontaneous Evolution: Our Positive Future (and a Way to Get There from Here)*. Countless other researchers have also made bridging science and spirituality their life's work.

In a certain sense, these scientific and spiritual messages form the basis for healing the myriad of other challenges in the world. If *Oneness* is an experience that transcends the mind—and if, when we experience Oneness, we feel a sense of connection with everyone and everything in existence—then does it not follow that we feel responsible for the well-being of everyone and everything? And does this not lead to positive action? Do we not then take steps to steward the Earth and heal ecological crises, including global warming? Do we not take steps to provide a basic level of well-being for each person on the Earth?

Every charitable cause, no matter how big or small, becomes important to us (though most families, out of necessity, will choose one or two causes to support). This is Oneness. Concerns for "the other" and the Earth become *our* concerns. If we are one with each person and all of life, and we are healthy and mature, do we not see our "self" as part of humanity and the entirety of the Earth? And do we not take responsibility for all of it and spring into action for at least part of it, particularly things we or our family feel deeply called to?

In a practical and tangible way, in a posture of Oneness, we take positive action and become the very thing Albert Einstein speaks about here, from his essay collection *The World As I See It*:

"A human being is a part of the whole called by us the universe, a part limited in time and space. He experiences himself, his thoughts and feelings as something separated from the rest, a kind of optical delusion of his consciousness. This delusion is a kind of prison for us, restricting us to our personal desires and to affection for a few persons nearest to us. Our task must be to free ourselves from this prison by widening our circle of compassion to embrace all living creatures and the whole of nature in its beauty."

Before we become overly excited about our prospects, let's consider what developmental theorists have warned us about concerning our ability to evolve.

Developmental theorists, including Don Beck, Clare W. Graves, and Ken Wilber, assert that most of the global population is not capable of fully understanding and expressing the Oneness I'm speaking of here. They share that at the most basic level of development, we are *egocentric*. Egocentric means: "I care only for myself."

Then, in our next state of evolution, we become *ethnocentric*. This means: "I care only for me and other human beings in my group/tribe/nation." Next, we become *world centric*. This means: "I care for all human beings regardless of race, color, sex, or creed—and even all sentient beings."

And finally, we become *cosmocentric*. This is the highest capacity for care and compassion and the pinnacle of moral development. At this stage, we feel connected to all forms of life on this planet and life beyond the borders of our solar system. Though developmental theorists tell us that most people in today's world—more than 70 percent—fall into either *egocentric* or *ethnocentric* worldviews, could the potential for feeling connected to all forms of life exist within us all?

At this point, you might ask, "Why bother?" If more than half the population is not capable of feeling connection, responsibility, and positive action for humanity and the world around us, why focus on planetary awakening and healing?

I like to look at the example of a family that includes a variety of older and younger members. By virtue of their age and experiences, some members are slower to understand and embrace family goals and ideas—yet this does not deter the older and more experienced members of the family from modeling more mature behavior to those who are less mature. In time, most families become consistently mature together and all members come to share those common goals and ideas.

Is there a reason why this process cannot work at community, state, national, and global levels? Mature, *world centric* and *cosmocentric* people exist all over the planet—so why not get started now? What are we waiting for?

Even if it feels like a tall order, this is the only way we can confront the existential crisis we face in today's world. Many people feel this way or are slowly coming around to this conclusion. Our own lives are important, of course; some of us have children, and new generations are being born into the world every year. And we obviously don't have the option (or the interest or financial means) to simply move to another planet, like Mars.

Saving the planet that is our current home is of tantamount importance.

For eighteen months after cutting my ties to the business world, the venture capital world, and the organizations that support them, I pondered questions like these. I tried to consider what my next steps might be. I wanted to do my best to raise awareness and help create the better world I felt certain was possible.

During this time, I subscribed to a free newsletter Neale Donald Walsch sent out regularly from his *Conversations with God* Foundation. One of the newsletters asked for responses from anyone who was applying the *Conversations with God* wisdom to their business. I sent a letter to the foundation and shared that I was doing exactly that and even attributed my company's growth to the spiritual principles I'd read in Neale's book.

A staff member passed my response along to Neale, who then reached out to me directly to ask if I'd be interested in coming up to Ashland, Oregon, to visit with him. I was delighted, and Stephanie and I packed our bags. During the visit, Neale talked about his ideas for expanding his reach and impact. I agreed to offer free consulting advice to him in those endeavors, so we were in touch regularly after that.

In one of our consulting conversations in the months that followed, Neale asked me if I'd be willing to fly up to Ashland again to lead the next planning session for his foundation. Once a year, Neale would gather with key members of his *Conversations with God* Foundation—as well as a few trusted friends from around the country—to chart the path for the coming year. His next planning session was just around the corner.

Neale had always led the planning sessions himself, but he recognized that it was hard to be a good facilitator and a contributor at the same time. He felt it would be better to be in one or the other roles. I told him I'd be happy to help.

The meeting took place over three days at a wilderness retreat in a beautiful forest setting near Ashland. Neale and his team were exceptionally focused and had much they wanted to address and accomplish. The meeting was quite spirited; people had strong opinions about what to do and how to best go about it. When Neale brought the proceedings to a close late Sunday afternoon, the group had made decisions. Everyone seemed grateful for the team's passion and commitment. It was a sign of things to come.

# 27
# FAMILY MATTERS
# (OUR SON DYLAN IS BORN)

Aside from consulting with Neale, my professional downtime was also a perfect opportunity for Stephanie and me to focus on having a family. Our attempts to do so had proved unsuccessful.

A friend introduced us to a potential surrogate mother who was open to carrying a child for us through artificial insemination. She was a wonderful person and we seriously considered expanding our family with her help, but Stephanie and I had both begun to feel we should adopt a child instead. We believed we could create a loving home for a baby whose birth mother might not be prepared to raise on her own.

We identified an adoption attorney and got the process started, and it wasn't long before we were matched with a pregnant woman in another state. In open adoption, the adoptive parents are present for the birth, along with the birth parents and their families. Stephanie and I arranged to fly across the country to be there. We were told it was going to be a baby girl, so we decided ahead of time to name her Karenna.

After the baby was born, however, the mother changed her mind and said that she wanted to keep her child. We knew that birth parents often change their mind once the baby is born. Giving up a child is a difficult choice to make.

We let the mother know that we completely understood. But privately, of course, we were heartbroken.

It was a long and emotional flight home to San Francisco, but even as difficult as it was, we knew we only wanted to adopt a child with the complete blessing and support of the birth parents and their families.

We were back to square one of the adoption process.

Then, amazingly, only six weeks later, we met another young woman who had also decided to give her unborn child up for adoption. She was just nineteen and lived in Las Vegas. She asked us to come there to meet her on Easter Sunday, and we made all the arrangements again.

As the expected delivery day approached, Stephanie and I drove to Las Vegas and got a room at a hotel near the hospital. On April 29, 2002, at ten p.m.—just as Stephanie and I were getting ready for bed—we got a phone call from the birth mother's family telling us she had gone into labor. They urged us to come to the hospital right away, so we jumped back into our clothes and drove over as fast as we dared.

The mother's whole family was there. We all spent the night together in her room, talking and waiting patiently until our son finally decided it was time to be born at five the next morning. Dylan was the name we'd chosen for him. Stephanie and I could hardly contain our excitement.

We needed to wait the twenty-four hours before we could take him back to the hotel with us, but the baby's mother and her family invited us to spend the day with them. We did, all taking turns holding Dylan and talking about how cute he was. We took him back to the hotel the next day as planned, and then drove home with him two days after that, once the final paperwork was signed. We had the full blessings of the birth mother and her family.

Just like that, we were parents!

As we were leaving our hotel in Las Vegas, we took the elevator down to the lobby with Dylan bundled up in Stephanie's arms. A woman on the elevator wanted to know how old he was. When we told her "four days," she looked at us quizzically and said, "And you've already taken him to Las Vegas?" Clearly, she thought we'd come there to gamble like everyone else and had brought our newborn baby along for the ride.

We chuckled about it all the way to the car.

# 28
# WHO WILL BE ON HUMANITY'S TEAM

In the spring of 2003, about a year after Dylan came into our lives, two things happened that influenced my path. The first was that Stephanie and I decided we wanted to adopt again. We'd always planned to have two children, so we contacted the adoption attorney again and began a new search in earnest. We knew it might not come together as quickly as it had the first time.

The second thing that happened was that Neale Donald Walsch invited me to fly up to his home in Ashland, Oregon, for three days to participate in a planning session for a new idea he had in mind. He said his goal was to discuss the idea with trusted friends he felt might add their critical insight. He hoped we might even want to be directly involved, if he decided to move forward with his idea.

I accepted the invitation, and a couple of weeks later, on the day of the meeting, I settled into a chair at Neale's house and looked around the room at the others he'd invited to attend. There were about twenty of us.

Neale explained that he wanted to launch a movement that would focus on our Oneness with the Divine, each other, and all of life. Untold numbers of organizations were already doing humanitarian and ecological outreach, he said, but none focused in a strategic way on what he saw as the root of humanity's problems: the illusion of separation. He had written in the *Conversations with God* series that mankind feels separated from the Divine, other humans, the animal kingdom, and the Earth itself. He said he wanted this movement to focus "narrow and deep" on that foundational disconnect.

In his book entitled *Tomorrow's God: Our Greatest Spiritual Challenge,* a *Conversations with God* book, which is part of his *Dialogue with God* series, Neale poses this question: "What would the world look like if we each deeply understood that we were offspring of the Divine, with no real borders between us, the Earth, and Life?"

Might we naturally heal our humanitarian and ecological crises? No longer would any of these problems be "out there" somewhere beyond our reach; they would be inside us. Solving the world's problems would then become as necessary as breathing.

Neale contends that we would heal the "optical delusion of consciousness" Albert Einstein spoke of, and "widen our circle of compassion to embrace all living creatures and the whole of nature"—just as the scientist suggested.

Here is an excerpt from that book:

GOD: "Live this message of non-separation, of the Unity of Life and the Oneness of All Things. Live it in a practical way, not merely in a conceptual way. Allow it to seep into your being at the deepest level and become a part of your subconscious and immediate response to every life encounter. Living this message is the best way to share this message. Then share it in other ways as well. Carry it to the world. Make it available to people."

NEALE: "We could form a team. We could call it Humanity's Team. Then we could ask people everywhere to create the space of possibility for a New Spirituality to emerge upon the Earth."

GOD: "That is an excellent idea. I invite you to do exactly that. If large numbers of people get together, create a team, and choose to experience conscious evolution, humanity could reach critical mass within a very short period. Decades, not centuries. Perhaps not even decades, but years. It is all up to you. It all depends on how you answer the call. It all depends on whether you even hear the call. For the soul of humanity calls out today, 'Who will be on humanity's team?'"

As Neale further explained his idea, which was certainly radical and revolutionary in 2003 when it first appeared, about a third of those participating in the planning session left after the first day, unable to get behind it.

In truth, I felt challenged—but I nonetheless believed I should be a part of it. Inside me, it felt like God was speaking to me directly, saying, "This is our moment. Who will stand with me?" God was inviting me to stand in truth and share my experience of the benevolent God I knew well, who was present in all of life. I wanted to explain my perception that God/Life are interchangeable, focused on that which is life-affirming, life-supporting, and life-enhancing.

Humanity's Team was the very thing I'd been waiting for since I'd left the corporate world behind.

Despite the deep calling I felt to become involved in this movement Neale wanted to create, I knew well that my friends—and even members of my own family—would not fully understand the messages. At that time, outside of mystical and deeply spiritual circles, there was little social acceptance for these ideas. I suspected that if I followed my heart and stepped forward to accept Neale's and God's invitation, I might lose decades-long relationships that were meaningful to me. But I'd obviously already crossed this bridge when I decided to leave the corporate world of Silicon Valley. I was well along a spiritual path now, and Neale's idea was unquestionably my next step on that journey.

Over the next two days of the planning session, I engaged fully in brainstorming ways to take this idea of his and make it a reality. At the end of the day on Sunday, when Neale asked if any of us were ready to sign on to help him with the nuts-and-bolts of developing and launching the Humanity's Team movement, only two of us stepped forward.

Prior to the actual launch, the other person fell out of alignment with Neale's vision. Neale offered me the volunteer job of leading the United

States wing of the organization on the spot, and without a second thought, I accepted. It was a big step, but I could hear my destiny calling.

# PART 3

## In Service to Humanity

# 29
# LAUNCHING A MOVEMENT

We had decisions to make. The planning session had been helpful in fleshing out possibilities along with the pros and cons of each. The planners had decided, after heated debate, that the movement would be open to everyone without charge instead of being a membership- or fee-based organization. I felt strongly that Humanity's Team should be free and open to the public.

The counter argument was that, if we didn't monetize the movement somehow, we'd have no budget for outreach or even to cover operating expenses. But I believed Humanity's Team could never grow into a true movement if we went down the fee-based path. It would limit our reach and impact. I felt certain it was better to launch the movement first and figure out how to financially support it later.

After more discussion, research, and inquiries, Neale and I officially launched Humanity's Team at a free event in June, 2003. The location was a well-known spiritual hub in Wilsonville, Oregon called The Living Enrichment Center.

Immediately after the planning session, I had formed a team to support me in my new role as head of Humanity's Team USA. Neale and his group worked on the global program, and my team and I started developing the program in the United States. We enlisted luminaries, authors, and experts in various fields to give presentations. We also planned for breakout groups and created space and time to meet and discuss ways to spread the global movement.

One of our speakers was Barbara Marx Hubbard, the author of the book *Conscious Evolution: Awakening the Power of Our Social Potential.*

I was standing in the crowd when Barbara was introduced at the June Humanity's Team launch, and most of the 800 people in attendance didn't recognize her. I heard people around me wondering aloud who she was—but by the time she finished her presentation, people were standing on their chairs shouting out in support of her message about conscious evolution. It was the last time Barbara attended a Humanity's Team event as an unknown to the crowd.

Prior to the event, we hung inspiring historical quotes in frames on the walls of The Living Enrichment Center, many of which still hang in my office today:

"The truth can never be wrong even if no one hears it." —Mahatma Gandhi

"When you cease to make a contribution you begin to die." —Eleanor Roosevelt

"Never doubt that a small group of thoughtful, committed citizens can change the world. Indeed, it's the only thing that ever has." —Margaret Meade

"You must decide—here and now, in these days and times, not in some far-off, distant future—whether the world is to be fashioned with tools of devastation or tools of recreation, with words of hate or words of hope, with acts of war or acts of peace, with thoughts of fear or thoughts of love." —from *The New Revelations,* a book in the *Conversations with God* series by Neale Donald Walsch

"Love is the energy which expands...opens up...sends out...stays... reveals...shares...heals." —from *Conversations with God: Book 1* by Neale Donald Walsch

Activists had arrived from around the world to participate in the Humanity's Team launch ceremony. Near the end of the event, Neale and I and our teams met with them to discuss how to best move forward. It was a wild meeting. This enthusiastic group raised diverse perspectives and ideas.

Neale and I shared that we felt the first step was to form a Humanity's Team Global Council that would meet again in three months—this time in Prague in the Czech Republic. Overall, the launch of Humanity's Team was an incredible success. We were on the map, and Neale and I were both committed to expanding the organization's growth and reach into every corner of the world.

For the meeting in Prague, Neale and I announced that we would create a volunteer Global Council to envision and oversee our activities. We invited people from all over the world to join us. When we arrived at a small hotel on the outskirts of Prague with the twenty-five others who had accepted our invitation, we were not surprised to find that the room consisted mostly of people from Europe.

Initially, the meeting got off track as we focused on creating teams, study groups, and operations centers. Spirituality is something that grows organically and authentically; it can't really be planned in a corporate way. Eventually, we got focused and started making progress.

Someone asked Neale what the New Spirituality was. Neale replied, "It is to renew and restore our connection with God and each other." His explanation resonated for me in a big way.

It was obvious that, at this early stage of Humanity's Team's growth, we needed to come together regularly. We decided to meet twice a year; the next meeting would be in May of 2004 in The Hague, Netherlands.

# 30
# A 'GOD JOB' IS BORN

On our way to the next meeting in The Hague, Neale and I stopped in Amsterdam for a day. After I settled into my hotel room, I decided to take a walk around the city without knowing where I was going. Quite by accident, I ended up in front of the home where Anne Frank had grown up in hiding, so I walked up the stairway to take the tour.

It felt very heavy, to say the least, to read about her short but inspiring life on the various plaques placed throughout the house. She had kept the famous diary of her experiences in the hidden annex where she and her family were protected for a time; they were eventually discovered and sent to a concentration camp, where Anne died at age fifteen.

As I wandered from room to room, I reflected on my own childhood and felt a new appreciation for the freedom, adventure, and growth I'd been able to enjoy during my formative years. I never once had to contemplate life-threatening situations or confinement or the possibility of death. Standing in the room where Anne Frank penned her diaries, I felt the stark contrast between her life and mine. I recognized how blessed I was to have grown up where and when I did.

Our Humanity's Team meeting took place two days later at the Stayokay hostel in The Hague. Once again, about twenty-five leaders joined Neale and me. They had come to share updates from their countries and to discuss plans for creating study groups and building Humanity's Team structures in their regions.

Most of the books in Neale's *Conversations with God* series had been released by that time, and they had profoundly impacted people all over the world. When word got out that Neale was going to be traveling to a location in Europe to work on spiritual programs, this stirred a great deal of interest.

It was quite an experiment to throw open the doors to anyone and everyone who wanted to represent Humanity's Team in their country. While they were excited about promoting the benevolent God described in Neale's books, they could not find consensus about how to work together or where we should focus to best accomplish our goals.

Everyone who attended the meeting clearly had their heart in the right place—yet there was no sense of vision-alignment and no notion for how we might achieve that alignment. The majority of the leaders wanted to create a decentralized movement so they could individually do anything they wished to do under its larger umbrella. In that way, each country could create its own vision, programs, and process for communicating with other countries.

In Europe, many spiritual people don't like to use the term "God." It is considered too malevolent and parochial, carrying too much baggage from the church of old. They associate the term with an angry and judging deity. Those who attended the meeting and felt this way advocated for not using the term "God" in any of the Humanity's Team messaging.

The lengthy ensuing dialogue around this idea was enthusiastic on all sides. In the end, the majority agreed that this was precisely why we were forming as a spiritual movement—to clear God's good name. We wanted the chance to prove God is not malevolent in any way or guilty of the ugly things often attributed to Him/Her by those with something to gain from instilling fear.

We were setting out to prove that God is benevolent and filled with love, grace, healing, and peace, and that God is indwelling, present in each person and all of life. Despite the majority decision, a few continued to push for stepping away from making references to God, even as we moved forward.

During our first thirty months as a movement, determining our process for organizing consumed much of our time. Should we create something entirely decentralized, so each country (and even community) could do anything it wished in the name of Humanity's Team? Or should we create a centralized spiritual movement to create global programs to be implemented uniformly?

Or should we create a mix of the two, with both centralized and decentralized features?

It seemed reckless to move ahead too far without all these details worked out. We needed to have a firm plan for what we wanted Humanity's Team to be and where we wanted to go. But with input from so many people who had different experiences in various cultures and faith traditions, what we ended up with was pandemonium.

I collaborated with a small team to sort all of this out and develop a strategy for moving forward. Neale was (and still is) an extremely busy author and speaker; between coordinating his speaking engagements, interviews, and other events, his foundation team was spread too thin. Neale realized it wasn't sustainable for him to continue to lead the global expansion of Humanity's Team.

During our meeting in The Hague, Neale asked if I'd be willing to step up my leadership responsibilities and become the Humanity's Team global director. He assured me that he'd remain on our council of trustees and provide enthusiastic support as a speaker, author, and in other ways when we called upon him, as his schedule allowed.

At that time, Humanity's Team had not yet formed a non-profit structure, developed a governance scheme, made plans for financial support, or put in place a process for managing its affairs. We didn't even have an official bank account. Everything we'd done so far had been supported by the few thousand a month Neale had solicited from donors.

And, as the meeting had proven, we hadn't yet even reached a consensus about what Humanity's Team mission would be or how we would operate.

I still felt sure, in my heart and soul, that this was the important work I had left Silicon Valley to do. After discussing Neale's request with Stephanie, I agreed to step into the larger leadership role Neale had offered me.

Stephanie and I had created the Farrell Family Charitable Fund in 2000, when we'd harvested a million dollars from the sale of her America Online stock. Over the years, I had continued to invest that money so it could multiply into even more financial capital to support our charitable work.

In the early years of Humanity's Team, I used these funds for the financial nurturing needed to launch and support our campaigns, create and maintain websites, secure an office space, create scholarships to help Global Council members get to annual meetings, and pay other vital expenses. Our staff was all-volunteer at that time, but we still needed money to support many critical functions. The Farrell Family Charitable Fund allowed us to keep moving forward.

Through these early years, Stephanie's mother, Ardy, had watched us launch the organization and begin to focus on trying to create a planetary awakening and a time of great flourishing for humanity. She heard us talking often about our wonderful and talented first group of volunteer team members and the devotion each of them was bringing to their job. She told me one day that she was sure the Divine was guiding us and called what we were doing a "God job."

In the moment, I thought it was a clever way to phrase it—but the deeper wisdom becomes more clear to me with every passing year. I believe God guided me to the program in New York where I first learned about AOL; that led to the investment that has made the Humanity's Team mission possible.

To this day, I and other members of the team continue to use the term "God job" to describe all the things we do to keep Humanity's Team's moving parts working as efficiently and effectively as possible. All the good things we're trying to accomplish in the world are "God jobs."

With the support of my small group of passionate and talented partners, Humanity's Team applied for non-profit status so we could formally organize activities and receive funds from those who resonated with our work and wanted to donate to us. Often, talented professionals have joined us at just the right time to allow us to grow to the next level of global impact.

One of these partners was Baya Beaudry, a certified management accountant with an MBA degree who was working for another non-profit when she attended the Humanity's Team launch in Oregon in 2003. We hired Baya for the volunteer position of "controller." She was invaluable in helping us apply to the IRS for 501(c)3 non-profit status. She also helped us in setting up our accounting systems, managing funds, and completing year-end reporting. Baya is still our chief financial officer today.

It wasn't until Humanity's Team entered its fifteenth year that we were finally able to begin to pay our frontline volunteers like Baya a slowly increasing stipend or small salary. We could finally take the first step in our trajectory toward being able to pay our critical team members more market-based salaries.

## 31
# A PERSONAL CHALLENGE AND A GIFT (OUR DAUGHTER SOPHIE IS BORN)

In August of 2004, I cracked a tooth on the right side of my mouth while eating trail mix with dry roasted nuts. As my dentist was repairing the tooth, he noticed a large protrusion on the side of my face. He felt sure I had a tumor and recommended that I see an ENT doctor at once.

The CT scan revealed a large parotid tumor. It was deep, near the base of my skull, and about the size of a golf ball—but the good news was, it was benign.

When the doctor told me how difficult the tumor removal would be, we found a surgeon at Stanford who routinely performed such complex surgeries. He recommended I arrange the surgery for a time when I could allow a full six months to recover. He told me I'd be able to resume administrative work within a few weeks, but warned I might experience temporary facial impairment and would be more comfortable staying out of public-facing events until things settled down.

The next Humanity's Team council meeting would be in November of that year, in Istanbul, Turkey. I decided to schedule the surgery for shortly after my return.

It had been almost a year since Stephanie and I had put ourselves out there as potential adoptive parents of another child. As I was preparing for my trip to Turkey and my surgery, we got a call from the mother of a pregnant girl in South Carolina who had found our profile on *adoption. com*. She said she hadn't intended to even look for adoptive parents in California, but while browsing the website, she'd accidentally clicked on California and saw our profile.

She told us that as soon as she read about us, she knew we were the right parents to raise her daughter's baby. She said her daughter would call us soon to confirm.

When she did call, it turned out not to be quite as simple as her mother had led us to believe. She was also only nineteen—just as Dylan's birth mom had been—and was only four months pregnant at the time. She also wanted to do her own research to find the perfect parents.

We resigned ourselves to the fact that she might choose someone else. But four months later, she called again while we were at the San Diego Zoo with Dylan. She explained that she'd looked through hundreds of profiles searching for the right adoptive parents but hadn't found a couple that felt right to her.

She said she'd finally come back to our profile and wondered if "sometimes mothers know best."

At this point, her baby girl was due in eight weeks. She asked if she could come out to visit us in California. She flew out and we had a great visit. Before she left, she told us she was now certain we should be her baby's adoptive parents.

Once all the paperwork was signed, we made plans to travel to where the birth mom was staying in St. Petersburg, Florida, so we could be present for our daughter's birth. As luck would have it, my brother Kevin lived nearby in Tampa, so we arranged to stay with him.

On October 15, 2004 at three in the morning, our daughter Sophie was born. Despite the late hour, we were there for the birth and during the small celebration we had afterwards, the nurses said Sophie looked just like a "China doll." She really did. She was perfect.

Shortly after Sophie was born, the birth mom and her family asked if they could be alone with Sophie for the rest of the day. Of course, we honored this request, but were extremely nervous because of what had happened with our first potential birth mom. We had to hold back our excitement about bringing Sophie home to join our family and steeled ourselves for the possibility that the birth mom might change her mind.

At around seven that night, she called to ask if we'd like to come back to the hospital to see Sophie before she went to sleep for the night. We felt a rush of relief, and everything went smoothly from there. We took Sophie back to my brother's house with us the next day, again with the full blessings of the birth mom and her family. It was a wonderful day.

This experience and others in my life have taught me that when I'm in situations where I don't have control over the outcome, the wise approach is to trust God and the universe. I try to believe God will bring about the outcome that is best for my growth and development, as well as the highest outcome for all who are involved. This way, the energy of my own thoughts won't interfere. Thoughts of fear and doubt can block the outcomes we desire by creating energy around outcomes that are the opposite of what we want.

As you encounter situations in your own life where you are nervous or afraid that things won't go the way you hope, I encourage you to make your intentions and desires crystal clear to God and the universe. Then simply stay centered and trust that you will receive the best possible outcome to serve your personal evolution toward your destiny.

# 32
# FOLLOWING MY TRUTH

The Humanity's Team Global Council meeting in Turkey was only a few weeks after Sophie's birth. I wasn't happy about having to be away from our new daughter, but I was thrilled that the meeting was to be at the

Boutique Saint Sophia hotel in Istanbul. It's walking distance to the Hagia Sophia Mosque and the Blue Mosque. Once again, this coincidence of the names felt divinely inspired.

Our agenda for the meeting was packed. We focused on exploring things we might do to create more deeply spiritual communities, but we found time to go to the mosques and the surrounding city. The meeting was highly productive. Neale joined us on Zoom on one of the days to hear what we were up to, and he shared ideas and inspiration with us.

When I returned from Turkey, my newly augmented family and my surgery procedure both awaited me. On the morning of the surgery, as one of the surgeon's assistants checked me in, he asked if I had any questions before going under the anesthesia.

I said, "It's just a routine surgery, so everything should be fine, right?"

"We hope so," the assistant said, "but this is a complex surgery. Things can go wrong. There's no way to be sure."

My surgeon had seemed confident the procedure would be routine. He gave me no reason for concern, aside from the inconvenient, six-month recovery period. I knew that fear was not a good place to be when going under anesthesia, so I settled myself and decided to proceed.

When I woke up afterwards, the doctor informed me that I had "inked margins." That meant small pieces of tumor tissue remained, but these might never become a problem of any kind. The nerve in the right side of my face had been affected; while the left side of my face had normal nerve functioning, the right side was temporarily paralyzed. I looked as though I'd had a stroke.

The surgeon's assistant said they had "ID-ed" my nerve following the operation, and it was alive and well. I'd just need to wait for the nerve to come back to normal function, and it would likely be fine again within that six-month span.

Unfortunately, it took longer to recover. I had to go about my life with an asymmetrical face for almost nine months.

I still recall walking into a Starbucks near my office in San Carlos, California, and the barista, who knew me, noticed my face. She asked what had happened to me with a look of abject shock and pity. I was embarrassed to have to explain, but it taught me an important lesson about feeling sorry for people. Her pity made me feel worse and more self-conscious than I already was. I vowed from that time forward to always offer compassionate assistance and support to others with disabilities or deformities—but to never outwardly show pity for them.

I still needed to decide whether to undergo radiation on the right side of my face, to minimize the chance of the tumor coming back. The surgeon wasn't sure it would be necessary, so in the end, I decided not to do it. Soon, the nerve began to function normally again, my face has remained healthy ever since.

As the final piece of the tumor puzzle, I sought out Christel Nani, a medical intuitive, to try to understand what might have been the root cause of the tumor. When she did my reading, she said that for years, I had refrained from fully sharing a truth that was vitally important to me. My silence had been like tying a balloon off while it was filling with air, forcing it to enlarge to dangerous levels. She told me I needed to fully share my truth if I wanted to ensure that the tumor never came back.

The moment she shared this with me, I understood exactly what had happened. Years earlier, when I was still a technology executive and involved in the Young Presidents' Organization, I had refrained from fully sharing my spiritual truths with those around me. I was as open about it as I felt I could be, but I had never fully revealed to others the full extent of my commitment to Oneness and my spiritual calling.

Fortunately, I'd chosen to leave that world where I could not be completely open about who I was and what was important to me. Now I realized how important it was for me to no longer hold that truth back, but to express it in every area of my life. It was further affirmation that I'd made a wise decision when I set out on my spiritual journey.

As if to underscore this new realization, things had become more challenging for me and my family. We were still living in Silicon Valley. In the 1990s, when ENS and Netigy were undergoing hypergrowth, the community often treated me like a rock star. Friends and neighbors were excited about what I'd achieved. They acted as though I knew something they didn't and was more important than them.

But all of that had changed. In our friends' and neighbors' minds, I'd clearly toppled from whatever pedestal people had put me on. At that time, money was the altar where everyone worshipped in Silicon Valley. It wasn't as though anyone had a problem with my spiritual focus and perspective— but I got the sense that people thought I'd lost my mind when I left the pursuit of the material world for a volunteer role in a spiritual movement.

I didn't feel supported in Silicon Valley professionally, and my family no longer felt at home there as we once had. Stephanie and I decided it was time to consider where we might want to live that better suited the people we had become since leaving our tech-world professions.

## 33
# A CIVIL RIGHTS MOVEMENT
# OF THE SOUL

In early 2005, Humanity's Team began to plan an International Conference at Bard College in Hudson, New York—ninety miles north of New York

City. The Institute of Advanced Theology at Bard had agreed to co-sponsor the event. Close to a thousand people from around the world—clergy and laypeople, scholars and students, professionals and laborers, business people and artists, policy makers and concerned individuals of many faiths and traditions—gathered with us for a three-day weekend in June.

This was outside the six-month recovery period from my surgery, so I should have been back to normal by then—but the facial nerve on my right side was still weak. My face on that side drooped badly and my neck was still bulging due to swelling from excess blood around the incision. I was embarrassed to show up at a public event in my condition, but there was nothing else I could do. One of the leaders attending the conference told me I looked like I'd been in a fight and the other guy got the best of me. It felt that way, too.

The conference itself was called "Seeds of Transformation: Toward a Spiritual Renaissance in a Time of Fundamental Change." We framed it like this: "The conference will reveal a trend in which people around the world inspect their spiritual beliefs, including ideas that we are better than others, that we are separate from one another, and in particular, that God wants it only one way on this Earth, and that we had better get it right or we are sure to be condemned."

We made it clear that the conference would explore the ramifications of the trend, as well as the fact that there were many paths to God, not just one. More than two dozen people spoke, including world-renowned authors, theologians, scientists, artists, and spiritual leaders of Eastern, Western, and Indigenous faiths. Lawrence Edward Carter Sr., the Dean of the Martin Luther King Jr. International Chapel at Morehouse College, was one of our featured speakers. Spiritual artist and leader Alex Gray also gave a presentation. We charged only $650 for those attending all three days, including all meals, which was just enough for us to break even on the cost of putting the conference together.

At our previous Global Council meeting, we'd decided that, from time to time, we would honor individuals for distinguished, inspired action and eminent visionary leadership. During the conference, we presented Neale Donald Walsch with our very first Humanity's Team Spiritual Leadership Award—a beautiful wood-and-brass plaque. It was more than fitting for Neale to be the first recipient. He had done so much to help us since the publication of the first *Conversations with God* book. He accepted the award graciously and with great humility.

To save money and encourage participation in the conference, we had also decided to set our next Global Council meeting to coincide with the international gathering. It had been two years since the launch of Humanity's Team, and it felt important to align our visions with the larger group on how we would govern ourselves and how we could best work together.

The meeting included charged emotional exchanges. We all deeply resonated with an inclusive New Spirituality focused on renewing and restoring our relationship with the Divine, each other, and all of Life. Yet there were differing opinions about how we should organize as a global movement to work and create projects together.

We knew we couldn't act on every idea at once. Finally, we agreed on which initiatives to tackle first. We hoped these would take us to the next level of visibility and impact.

Following the meeting, I arranged for the key members of our support team to meet in Northern California at the Hidden Villa Hostel in Los Altos Hills, to discuss how we might forge a tighter and more effective relationship. I sought help from a friend from my Young Presidents'

Organization days, Dr. Ichak Adizes. Adizes had been an invaluable resource to the Northern California YPO chapters.

His company, Adizes International, had created a model based on mutual trust and respect to help organizations work together more effectively—and that was exactly what we needed. We didn't have a budget, so I asked Dr. Adizes if he would be willing to offer pro-bono consulting assistance. He agreed and dispatched one of his key workshop leaders to join our planning session.

We even had a little beyond-coincidence moment of validation during the drive to Hidden Villa for the meeting when we noticed a car had come up behind us with a California license plate that read: "GODINU." We laughed and took it as a sign that we were on the right path, and that good things were just ahead.

During the Adizes workshop, we focused on our visions for the future, reviewed plans that we'd previously agreed upon, and talked about how our relationships with each other had evolved from working closely together. Even though we'd only been a "team" for a little more than two years, we'd made important progress and were beginning to develop the kind of trust that would be necessary to accomplish the goals we'd set.

This was a critical moment for Humanity's Team. Our governance agreement called for 75 percent of the council to approve any steps. But as recently as our previous meeting, members of the group had continued to push for a more decentralized structure and more autonomy.

If we could not reach an accord, I knew Humanity's Team might cease to exist.

Thankfully, the workshop brought us all into closer vision alignment. It also made us tighter as a team. We could all feel that we'd had a breakthrough. By the end of the first day, we decided it was time to create an official "Statement of Direction" to strengthen the effectiveness of Humanity's Team as an active, coordinated spiritual movement.

The following day, we began in earnest discussing and drafting a statement that we hoped would improve our interaction, ensure vision alignment, provide structure, improve coordination, and inspire team resonance—ambitious goals, to say the least.

The draft we created during the workshop underwent changes over the next few months. When we finally brought it to a vote, the Global Council—which at that time consisted of our support team, the country coordinators, and me—overwhelmingly approved the proposal by a vote of thirty-one to one. We called it, simply, "The November 29th, 2005 Statement of Direction." It became the framework for everything we've done since that time.

Here's what our Statement of Direction affirms:

On this day, November 29th, 2005, we hereby formally declare that...

- Humanity's Team is an active, coordinated spiritual movement with uniform and unifying programs worldwide (allowing for community and cultural differences).
- Humanity's Team is always creating the space for the emergence of the New Spirituality.
- Humanity's Team is open and transparent in its operation and finances.
- Humanity's Team always operates with the knowingness that we are all One.
- Humanity's Team is a Global Movement (a Civil Rights Movement for the Soul).

- Humanity's Team uses **The Five Steps to Peace** from "The New Revelations," in Neale Donald Walsch's *Conversations with God* as the anchor in all we are being and doing:

Peace will be attained when we, as human beings...

1. **Permit** ourselves to acknowledge that some of our old beliefs about God and about Life are no longer working.
2. **Explore** the possibility that there is something we do not understand about God and about Life, the understanding of which could change everything.
3. **Announce** that we are willing for new understandings of God and Life to now be brought forth—understandings that could produce a new way of life on this planet.
4. **Courageously** examine these new understandings and, if they align with our personal inner truth and knowing, enlarge our belief system to include them.
5. **Express** our lives as a demonstration of our highest beliefs, rather than as a denial of them.

We included the Five Steps to Peace in the Statement of Direction because even if we aren't all overtly religious, most of us grew up in families with some open beliefs about God and about life—beliefs that, in many cases, were passed down from generation to generation with blind acceptance and no reevaluation. Within many of those belief structures, there is the idea that God stopped talking to us thousands of years ago, as well as a belief that God wants us to stay in line out of fear.

Because of those mischaracterizations, Humanity's Team encourages everyone to deeply consider the following questions:

- What if there is no separation between us and God, and He/She is talking to us all the time?
- What if our conscience and imagination are actually God's inspiration?
- What if God's relationship with us is loving and doesn't call upon us to fear Him/Her?
- What if we lived our lives as a demonstration of our highest and grandest beliefs?

Shortly after the creation of Humanity's Team, Neale described us in one of his *Conversations with God* books as being "A Civil Rights Movement of the Soul." We can ascribe different meanings to this. In today's world, the mind and body get the majority of the attention, while the soul has been treated as having lesser importance. As a result, we get so caught up in our intellectual, emotional, and physical lives that we lose touch with what the inner voice of our soul is calling us to do.

Part of Humanity's Team's mission is to encourage people to spend time in stillness and silence each day, so that we can hear our soul's calling and follow where it leads. When we do this daily, even for a short time, we remain in touch with what is instinctual deep within us. Then we come back into our true essence—our true self.

The soul—in humans, animals, and the Earth—is largely ignored by global society. Our bodies are given certain civil rights, but our souls receive little acknowledgement. Humanity's Team, in its "Civil Rights Movement for the Soul," invites us to reorder our priorities so the soul becomes both a larger focus of our attention and a more prominent part of our daily lives.

I truly can't encourage you enough to regularly renew your own sense of connection to the Divinity of the natural world—including animals, both domestic and in the wild—by going outdoors and focusing on the beauty at every level of Life. Whether you are hiking, working in your garden, petting a dog or cat, or observing birds and other wildlife in any of their natural behaviors, it's best not to think about other aspects of your life at this time. Set aside your current challenges and concerns.

Instead, focus on what you experience during these kinds of practices, this will center your energy and make you better equipped to deal with those daily challenges when you return.

## 34
# BIRTHING BIG PLANS IN KYOTO, JAPAN

We invited other countries to host our Global Council meeting each year. We decided we'd meet in Kyoto, Japan, for our May, 2006 meeting. Global Council members from the United States, Europe, Africa, and South America were present, and Neale also joined us.

The Japanese team were exceptional Global Council hosts. They arranged ceremonies with swords, local traditions, and meditation at local Shinto shrines and Buddhist temples. They also arranged for a special outing to visit Mount Kurma, the birthplace of Reiki practice. It was truly special to hike to the mountain top, where there is a shrine, and then over the mountain to the Reiki temple.

This was our first meeting since we'd created the Statement of Direction, and it was immediately clear that we were unified as a team in ways we had not been before. Everything went smoothly. We engaged in team-building activities such as creating playful skits together, and we also planned a world tour for 2007 to take the messages of Humanity's Team out to any country willing to host a tour stop.

115

We tentatively set the World Tour dates for March 23 to April 29, 2007 and named the tour, "Around the World in Oneness: The Humanity's Team 2007 World Tour." We all had so much to do when we got home! Our country coordinators agreed to be the hosts and promoters in their individual countries—something they had not done before—and Neale and I agreed to speak alongside other speakers invited by the coordinator in each country. Stephanie and I agreed to partially subsidize each of the host countries.

In our grassroots promotions, we emphasized the idea that "We Are All One." We believed this was the message all of humanity desperately needed to hear and embrace.

We presented We Are All One as an answer to some big questions:

- What is the ONE idea that can end all violence in the world?
- What is the ONE idea that can build a lasting peace between diverse cultures?
- What is the ONE idea that can end hunger and poverty on every continent?
- What is the ONE idea that can restore our planet's environment?

The Around the World in Oneness World Tour had ambitious intentions. The first was to raise awareness of humanity's Oneness. We wanted to declare that, if we were to collectively embrace the belief that we are all one—with each other, with all of life, and with God/the Universe/Divinity—the world would see a major shift in the way individuals and entire societies behaved. This is truly the foundational first step toward creating a world of compassion, harmony, and peace. This is how we can change the tide of global events.

It was also our intention to officially announce across the globe that Humanity's Team was an active, coordinated worldwide movement with more than 15,000 members—the number of people on our email list at the time—operating in more than ninety countries. We invited anyone who resonated with our mission to join us for free and be of service to everything we hoped to accomplish.

The tour was also the vehicle for the launch of our Worldwide Oneness Campaign, our five-year commitment to reach out to individuals and organizations across the globe—including the United Nations—to generate support for adopting the "We Are All One" platform as a global primary organizing principle.

We designed the Oneness Campaign to explain what Oneness is and is not. We wanted people to deeply consider how diversity and unity fit together perfectly. Although there is ample ancient wisdom out there telling us we are all one, we know from our observations and life experiences that we are each unique, with our own gifts and talents. Even when we awaken to unity and Oneness, these differences are not diminished. Instead, our gifts, our talents, our character, and our contributions become wonderful puzzle pieces that can fit together beautifully in the mosaic of Oneness and unity we call life.

There is a natural and healthy tension between the idea of Oneness and the idea of individuality. Not everyone gets this idea, and some push back against it. We might fear we will lose our sense of self and our identity. When we talk about Oneness, we need to make it clear that we are not talking about being absorbed into a unity that causes us to lose our individual identity. In fact, Oneness and individuality are not mutually exclusive at all.

In the United States, for example, states do not lose their individual identities but instead bring their diverse landscapes, cultures, and contributions to the whole. Things can be unified without having to be "sameified." Each state has its own rich and beautiful contributions, expressions, and history—but at the same time, those diverse states joined together in a single nation.

We were determined to spread this message everywhere. We hoped to raise awareness, spark discussion, and eventually inspire a movement toward conscious living worldwide.

# 35
# BUYING OUR DREAM HOME

As our World Tour approached, it was time to extend an invitation to everyone who might want to join us in all the countries we'd be visiting. We created a flyer that said, "Are you in for this next great adventure for our species?" and "If you'd like to support us in any way, please do contact us. We look forward to having you on board!"

After making all the arrangements at each of the tour's ten stops, we scheduled the forty-day tour. We would fly west around the world, starting in New Zealand and concluding in Canada. Not only was this a monstrous task to plan, but it was only one element of my life's mounting complexity.

Stephanie and I had decided to move from Northern California to Boulder, Colorado in May, just two weeks after the completion of the tour.

In February of 2007, we visited Boulder on our final house-hunting trip. The Humanity's Team world tour was set to begin in forty-five days, and we had to be out of our Bay Area home only forty-five days after that. It was imperative that we make an offer on a home during this Colorado trip.

To complicate matters, Boulder was hit by a huge snowstorm the day we arrived. We rented the largest four-wheel-drive vehicle we could find to make sure we could get around without getting stuck. But the timing of our visit was good, as real estate sales had already started to slow in Boulder, as if they were anticipating the economic recession that would begin just a few months later.

We eventually found a home we loved. The building wasn't quite finished and it was above our price range, but we knew the sellers were motivated. We made an offer well below the asking price. It was all we felt we could comfortably afford. After a couple of days had passed, we still hadn't heard back from the builder. We felt sure the owners had rejected our offer.

We were scheduled to fly back to the Bay Area the following day, so we instructed our real estate agent to set up a meeting with the owner of another, smaller property, close to the home we liked. We intended to make an offer to rent this home for a year, since we hadn't found anything to buy yet. We knew Boulder was where we wanted to be.

The next day, an hour before we had to leave for the airport, we stood in the rental home reviewing the contract at the kitchen table. Just as we were about to add our signatures, Stephanie's cell phone rang. It was our real estate agent; the owner of the other house had accepted our offer!

The house was only a couple of blocks away, and the builder was heading there to meet us. We called the airline to switch to a later flight, to give us time to get the paperwork signed.

As I mentioned, the home wasn't finished yet. The upper floors were fully built out and only needed carpet, but the basement still had a cement floor. We agreed on a slightly higher price with the understanding the basement would be finished with the same level of trim and attention to detail as the main and second floors had been. We were in such a hurry, that we didn't fully even understand all the home's features. Months later, when we returned to Boulder to move in, we learned our new place had solar power, radiant heat in the courtyard and driveway, and other features we hadn't been aware of.

Boulder had created an incentive program called "The Green Point Program for New Construction," so the home had been built in an environmentally friendly way with sustainable components, including above-code energy efficiency for lighting and air sealing. No old-growth timber was used. One of the garages included an electric vehicle-charging station. Even the landscaping was designed for sustainability.

The house is truly wonderful and one of a kind, and it has been the perfect home for our family for many years. If Stephanie's cell phone had rung minutes later, it would have been too late; we'd have signed the paperwork for the rental house. Perfectly timed blessings have arrived so often since I began serving Humanity's Team.

# 36
# AROUND THE WORLD IN FORTY DAYS

We had purchased a new home! Now we had only ninety days before we were planning to move in—and those ninety days would be busy for me. The Humanity's Team world tour would be circling the globe for forty of those days. We still had so much planning to do before the first leg of the trip began in late March.

As I prepared to leave for the tour, Stephanie impressed upon me the enormous amount of work we had to do getting ready for our move to Colorado. She was caring for Dylan and Sophie, who were still just five and two and a half at the time. With all that we needed to do, I realized I could not afford to be gone for almost six weeks on the tour. I decided to skip the first two stops. This cut the trip down to a more manageable four weeks for me.

The woman who had volunteered to be our host for the tour stop in Lisbon, Portugal, was Maria Ribeiro Ferreira. She had been present at our very first Global Council meeting in Prague in 2003 and had served on the Humanity's Team Council of Trustees with Neale and me for years. She remains a good friend. She had arranged a wonderful venue for us to use. About 600 people attended the evening program.

We had asked our tour hosts to schedule the events with me leading off and speaking for thirty minutes, followed by Neale for sixty minutes. Neale is a professional public speaker whose style is to speak in the moment, so he didn't have to do much preparation ahead of time. On the other hand, I was accustomed to carefully planning and preparing for public speaking engagements, so I spent about a month scripting my presentation and then memorizing it so I could look at my audience while I spoke, without the need for a lectern or stand of any kind. I then practiced my talk aloud, both alone and in front of Stephanie.

Humanity's Team is foundationally about living in loving expression through service, so my talk brought in a recent incident that had happened in New York City involving a man named Wesley Autrey. The media had dubbed him the "Subway Samaritan." Wesley had leaped down onto the subway tracks to save the life of Cameron Hollowpeter, a film student who suffered a seizure and tumbled from the platform onto the tracks below. Autrey saw him fall just as the lights of an oncoming train appeared in the tunnel, rushing toward them.

Autrey didn't have enough time before the train arrived to haul the semi-conscious Hollowpeter back onto the platform, so he rolled the fallen man into the drainage ditch between the tracks, then lay down in the ditch with him just as the train pulled in.

121

The subway engineer had seen what was happening and slammed on the brakes, but he couldn't stop in time, and all but two of the cars passed over the two men. When they crawled out from beneath the train, the only damage to either of them was some grease on Autrey's cap.

Autrey insisted in the press that he was not a hero and that he had just done what anyone would do. I felt the story was a wonderful opportunity to talk about the fact that our basic human instinct is to preserve life, even at the risk of our own, rather than mere self-preservation.

The audience appreciated the presentations from all the speakers that night, and the feedback we heard afterward proved to me that the tour was having an impact on people and raising awareness in just the way we had hoped.

During the question-and-answer session that followed the presentations, someone in the audience asked if we were "a religion or a cult." This was a wonderful opportunity to share that we did not in any way hold ourselves and our beliefs above others, and that we encouraged everyone to "go within" to find out if their own truth resonated with all we had shared.

Oneness means there is no separation, and the Divine expression is always the highest thought, the clearest word, and the grandest feeling, which we call *love*.

## 37
# FACING CHALLENGES DURING THE TOUR

The next stop on the tour was Moldova, a country in the northeastern corner of Europe's Balkan region. Moldova had declared its independence from the Soviet republic only sixteen years earlier, so Soviet-style architecture dominated urban areas including the city of Chisinau, where we were holding our event.

When I checked into my hotel, it was deserted. It was like being in a ghost town. I only saw one other person throughout the whole check-in process and the walk to my room: a woman wearing a short skirt and a T-shirt with the English word "Sex" on it. Only later did it dawn on me that she was a prostitute working for the hotel. The city was obviously economically depressed, and I suspected, sadly, that many citizens had few ways to bring money into their lives other than sex work.

During the entire tour, we only ever had one heckler during the presentations—and that happened to be in Moldova. The presentation itself was already challenging enough; I had to speak much more slowly than usual so the interpreter could hear me clearly and then translate my words.

The moment I began, a man in the third row began calling out, loudly, and in Moldovan—which of course, I couldn't understand—seeming intent to cause a disruption. He waved his arms repeatedly, trying to get my attention. His taunting was incredibly distracting, causing me to lose my concentration more than once.

This was a reminder to me that our message of a loving God, and the idea of Oneness with all of life, might be considered radical and even dangerous by people who neither sense the truth of it nor embrace its foundational power.

Neale's *Conversations with God* series of books were all worldwide bestsellers that had influenced people everywhere we went. Many were still not sure what to make of the extraordinary insights contained in the books, which we saw firsthand during the tour.

Several readers mistook Neale for the *source* of the profound wisdom in the answers to the questions Neale asks in the *Conversations with God* dialogues. They treated him as a prophet rather than "an ordinary guy having an extraordinary experience," as Neale himself describes it. Neale has always maintained that the answers did not come from him, but *through* him from the Divine.

Our next stretch of stops on the tour would see us speaking three times in five days, first in England for about 500 people; then in Germany, for about the same number; and then in Johannesburg, South Africa, to an audience of about 1,000.

Until Johannesburg, my presentations had been well-received at all tour stops. I felt I'd been able to give people a clear sense of the work we were doing in spreading our messages of Oneness and unconditional love. The feedback from both organizers and participants was positive. But then something odd happened.

During my presentation, I suddenly felt "wooden," as though I was in a play and merely mouthing the words rather than experiencing and transmitting the emotion in my message. I realized I had over-rehearsed the speech. After delivering it four times at the previous tour stops, I was now just robotically saying the words.

It was obvious to me that the audience could sense this disconnect, too, and I finished to only a light smattering of applause. I felt terrible about this. My piece of the program was meant to convey important messages; now I feared they hadn't been received. I felt I'd let everyone down.

Afterward, I walked dejectedly over to the vendor island and sat down in one of the chairs where local masseuses were giving free massages. After a therapist worked on my tight muscles, I was finally able to relax and release my disappointment. I regained my composure by vowing I'd get my message across every time, from then on.

Our next tour stop was in Buenos Aires, but the event was a full week away. I decided to make use of the down time by writing a whole new script for the Buenos Aires audience. I didn't want to risk repeating the experience I'd had in Johannesburg. Creating an entirely new presentation was quite a challenge. I'd had a month to create and practice the first one, and now I had to try to squeeze that process into a single week.

Fortunately, I was able to get into a good flow with the writing and practicing, and the proof came when I spoke before more than a thousand people in Buenos Aires. Their feedback was all positive.

Our next stop was in Atlanta, Georgia. This was our only tour stop in the United States and the last stop before our final event in Canada. The presentation I created for Buenos Aires had been unique to that location; now I felt I needed to create another brand-new presentation, to try to better connect with Americans and Canadians. This time, I had only five days before the event! Somehow, I managed to finish the new script and memorize it in time.

Unfortunately, there was yet another challenge in Georgia.

An enthusiastic group had worked on planning and organizing the U.S. tour stop. When they told us they were planning to rent a large, four-star hotel meeting room in downtown Atlanta, we urged them to consider something a bit more modest. We knew we'd be unlikely to fill such an expensive venue. In the end, we couldn't dissuade them. The expenses for that event exceeded the revenue and scholarship amount.

This was a difficult lesson, but it showed us that moving forward, we needed to be more conservative when organizing Humanity's Team activities.

Two days later, we wrapped up our world tour in Vancouver, Canada. The event was in a more modest location, and it was nearly filled to capacity. Everything went smoothly for the final presentations. We all agreed that we had been successful in our mission to extend our global reach and impact, and we felt this was a sign of good things ahead.

Many people now had a better understanding of the idea that we are all One with the Divine, with each other, and with life—and that the Divine is non-judgmental, unconditionally loving, and supportive on every level. What we had done over the previous forty days had given them this understanding. We all felt the world tour had raised the bar, if only a little.

It might be easy to assume we were trying to climb too steep a hill with our goals. But researchers from Rensselaer Polytechnic Institute have found that when just 10 percent of a population holds an unshakable belief, the majority of that society will eventually adopt that belief. This fact, and the joy we experienced from the work we were doing, gave us the drive to continue our mission—even though the worldwide change we were working toward was not yet in sight.

## 38
# LIVING THE MESSAGES OF NON-SEPARATION

Only two days after I'd unpacked from the tour, the moving vans arrived to pack up everything in our house to take it to our new home in Boulder. Stephanie had lived in Northern California her whole life, except for her years attending the University of Colorado in Boulder. I'd lived in the Bay Area since arriving there, right out of college. It was especially difficult to say goodbye to Stephanie's parents, Charlie and Ardy. We invited them to fly out to visit us as often as they were willing to come.

Once we arrived in Boulder and had settled in, our mixed feelings about leaving California quickly dissipated and we knew we'd made the right decision. At the time of our move, the Bay Area had a population of a little over 6 million. Boulder City had only 100,000 residents; the whole county had a population of about 300,000. Driving around town, parking, and making appointments was a piece of cake here compared to our old neighborhood, and we discovered a large, conscious group of people who were clearly committed to ecological preservation and communing with nature. We felt right at home in our new house and our new community!

That year, 2007, the Humanity's Team annual Global Council meeting was to take place in Lisbon, Portugal, just around the corner from where we had presented during our world tour. The meeting was in June, so I had to head out the door again shortly after we arrived in Boulder.

The council in Lisbon acknowledged that they could still feel the incredible energy and momentum we'd created during the world tour. We were not professional organizers or promoters by any means, but our team had somehow pulled it off. We'd circled the globe, stopping in ten cities in forty days.

Now we were looking for the most effective way to create a larger global movement.

In Neale's book *Tomorrow's God,* we are invited to "Live the message of non-separation, of the Unity of Life, and the Oneness of Things, in a practical way." Neale wrote that we could achieve critical mass in a short period … not even decades, but years.

This emphasizes that really living the message as individuals is the most important thing we can do. This alone could create a tipping point, when enough of us accept and commit to the calling. But as the Global Council discussed this idea, we all felt we could do more to encourage people to work collectively toward that goal.

One of the program ideas we came up with was called "Celebration of Life"—a chance for people to come together to revere and celebrate the Divine and life itself. The foundational focus would be on God as benevolent, unconditionally loving, and absolutely good, and on the idea that because people and all of life exist within that one Divine energy, all people and all of life are also inherently good.

We agreed in Portugal that getting programs like these off the ground was our next big step toward creating the kind of movement that could have a global impact. We also knew that there was no guarantee that the kinds of programs we imagined would be successful.

Sometimes a new program works and grows into something thriving. Other times, for whatever reason, it doesn't quite come together. In this case, the "Celebration of Life" program didn't work. We realized one reason was that there were already religious and spiritual organizations centered around that same foundational belief.

We clearly needed something a bit more fresh and original.

## 39
# CREATING COMMUNITY

When I returned to Boulder, Stephanie and I were still so new to the area that we had much to do before we could become fully immersed in the culture of our new home city. Humanity's Team itself was not yet known to leaders in the Boulder area, so I planned a reception at my home to introduce our organization and activity to the city's business and political leaders. Neale agreed to fly out to join us for the event.

I needed help preparing for the reception, so I recruited people from the Denver/Boulder/Fort Collins area. The local team I had put together helped me get my home ready for the event, and they also reached out to Coloradoans they felt might resonate with our work. Spiritual pioneer Rabbi Zalman Schachter-Shalomi and mediator William Ury were among those who agreed to attend. We also met separately with Mo Siegel, one of the cofounders of Celestial Seasoning.

Neale made a tremendously positive impression on everyone at the reception. The event helped to seed Humanity's Team in Colorado in wonderful ways that have continued to unfold.

At that time, everyone who was part of Humanity's Team was still a volunteer, including me. We'd all agreed to pay for our own workstations, cell phones, and supplies. While most religious organizations get financial support from their members, spiritual organizations—especially virtual ones like Humanity's Team—can't consistently count on donors for support.

My first office in Boulder was a mile and a half from my home in the back of an executive suite behind a shopping center. My two small rooms were reasonably priced, and we had good parking and many restaurants nearby, which was handy for lunch meetings.

After I'd been there a few years, the landlord shocked me by asking me to move. A bigger company was taking over the rest of the executive suite and needed my offices as well. I mentally accepted this, although I dreaded finding a new office with a longer commute.

As an afterthought, I asked if he knew of another available office nearby. He took me to the other side of the shopping center, where we saw a space with fresh paint, lots of light, and huge windows that looked out on mature Austrian Pine trees. Before I let myself get too excited, I asked him the price. He said I could have it for the same amount I had been paying!

This was yet another example of guidance, blessings, and support arriving at the moment when it is most needed. This theme has played out often during my Humanity's Team journey.

Meeting such challenges has helped me to grow as a person and as a leader, making me better prepared for the next challenges that arise. It has strengthened me spiritually and mentally.

Part of doing spiritual work means taking time to breathe, trust, have faith, and allow God/Source/the universe to take care of the rest.

## 40
# PERSEVERING THROUGH BIG CHALLENGES

Sometimes challenges arrive in our lives completely out of nowhere, blindsiding us and changing whatever trajectory we thought we were on. Our first reaction is often, "Why me?" But these challenges often deliver unexpected benefits that are not readily apparent.

If only it were easier to remember that fact while challenges are unfolding.

Shortly after moving into our new home in Boulder, both Stephanie and Dylan began to experience unexpected health issues. Stephanie had always been in great shape, but quite unexpectedly, her weight ballooned up forty pounds. She hadn't changed her diet or exercise routine at all. At the same time, Dylan became inexplicably irritable and short-tempered. He began to show signs of being emotionally distressed.

We were new to Colorado, so we weren't sure what might be at the root of these sudden changes. We wondered if our living environment could be to blame. Initially, we thought it might be the low humidity level in the home during the winter months; we weren't yet accustomed to the high, dry climate. But adding a humidifier didn't seem to help. We started looking into other possibilities.

The interior wood on the floors, doors, and areas of paneling in our new home were finished with oil-based stains; could this have caused these health problems? We stayed at a hotel for two weeks while a contractor sanded the stain off the floors and replaced it with a water-based stain. These stains have come a long way and are still beautiful without releasing volatile organic compounds (VOCs) into the air.

While the new stain looked great, Stephanie and Dylan still seemed to be getting worse. We didn't know that it was something in the house, but we decided that Stephanie should move into a hotel for a more extended period, to see if that helped her regain her health while we investigated our new house more closely. The kids took turns staying with her at a nearby hotel for the few months this project dragged on.

We had brought in professionals to help figure out what the problem might be, even before we sanded off the oil-based stain. Now we hired specialists to test everything we could think of. We started with the repurposed, 150-year-old beams that stretched across ceilings throughout the house. They had come from an old barn in Pennsylvania. While they were beautiful to look at, the beams tested positive for mold contamination. We tried to save the beams with thorough cleaning, but it didn't work. They needed to be replaced.

Another specialist discovered that cardboard packing had been left in the high-velocity air conditioning and heating unit on the second floor of the house, where all the bedrooms were. Mold on that cardboard had been blown into every room on that floor. Even the plastic duct hoses were contaminated. Most of the unit and all the hoses had to be replaced. That meant opening the walls and ceilings.

Decontaminating the house was an incredibly expensive and time-consuming project. We even had to bring a crane inside the house to extract the large beams. Contractors estimated it would take six months to complete all the work, plus another three months to eradicate mold from the parts of the house that were salvageable.

That meant we needed to lease somewhere else to live for at least nine months.

I had never been involved in a lawsuit. I'd always preferred talking things out when conflicts arose, so I tried that first. I met with the contractors who sold us the home and the subcontractors who installed the A/C and heating system. Together, we reviewed all the information I'd gathered. I told them we were not seeking injury compensation for the problems but wanted a fair and equitable arrangement to solve the issues; we would only look for legal remedies if we couldn't agree on a settlement.

Both parties were apologetic and not at all defensive. After discussing the situation back and forth, we agreed upon a settlement that would allow us to move forward.

Stephanie and I then began our search for a temporary residence so the work on our house could begin in earnest. We decided that we just needed something functional for the four of us; the most important factor was that the temporary home needed to be free from mold and toxins and have a top-notch ventilation system. After reviewing available properties, we settled on a home in the Newlands area that was only a mile from downtown Boulder and close to the Rocky Mountain foothills.

The 1940s-style home had been recently repainted and decorated with clean, functional, non-allergenic carpet, rugs, and furniture. The owners were allergy sensitive, so they had taken great care to assure the home would support holistic health.

The house was much smaller and simpler than ours; in fact, it was much like the one I'd grown up in. The bedrooms were close together and the living room was a good space for gathering and conversation. We were always in sight and earshot of each other, which helped us maintain a comforting sense of family during this challenging time. We were all grateful to be together again in a healthy home environment.

While we all managed to remain in good spirits through this upheaval, it was awkward not knowing when we'd be able to move back into our home. We still didn't know if Stephanie and Dylan would be able to live there comfortably after what they'd been through, but we felt confident that if they didn't feel good about it, we could easily sell the home. We trusted that the Divine was guiding us and that we would eventually land where we were meant to be.

When the remediation project on our home was at last complete, we crossed our fingers and hoped for the best. To our relief, both Stephanie and Dylan's health continued to improve, as it had during our time in the rental house. Dylan became less irritable, and Stephanie felt like her body was on its way back to normal.

During the trying time with our new house, my Humanity's Team colleagues began referring to me as "Job" from the Bible. As the story goes, Job endures great suffering in unusual ways for years on end, without understanding why. Job somehow manages to maintain his happiness through following "passions engaged by the enormity of God." Eventually, God restores his normal life and prosperity.

I could look at what had happened to me and my family as a "trial" in the same way, since we had felt guided to find and buy that house. So why did these problems surface, creating unforeseeable health and financial hardships for my family?

Many people might assume that the universe was trying to tell us we were headed in the wrong direction by placing an obstacle in our path. But everything changed for me the moment I shifted the focus of my life from earning more money and having more personal success, to finding more meaning and creating more fulfillment. With that change of priorities from the material to the spiritual—and from enriching myself to enriching others—I began to see experiences such as the one I've just recounted not as *opposition* but as *opportunity*. In other words, the problems weren't there to block me, but to motivate me and help me to grow.

People often feel blessed when good tidings arrive in their lives but then victimized when trouble begins. Through the process of conscious evolution, however, we can begin to see that everything ultimately works for our benefit—even though it might not look like it while a particular experience is unfolding.

I know of more than one person who has endured what they felt was one of the worst things that could ever happen to them, such as being fired, losing a relationship, or being uprooted by circumstances. Then later, they described that event as one of the *best* things that ever happened to them.

In Neale Donald Walsch's *Conversations with God* books, this is called the Law of Opposites: The moment we make any major choice, the exact opposite of that choice will arise in our awareness. It must happen in order for us to experience what we wish to experience.

It's important to be aware of the Law of Opposites when you're considering a major change in priorities and purpose.

To offer a simple example, we cannot experience being "tall" unless our awareness includes the experience of "short." We cannot experience "big" without the existence and the awareness of "small." The term "fast" has no meaning without an awareness of something we call "slow."

The sudden arising, then, of conditions, circumstances, or events that appear to be blocking us can sometimes simply be life's invitation to learn more about the opposite of what we think we want. This allows us to experience more fully what we choose.

There's a reason why so many great spiritual traditions bring us the message: "Judge not, and neither condemn." There's a reason spiritual masters also say, "Raise not your fist to heaven, and curse the darkness not, but be a light un*to* the darkness, that you might know who you really are."

I hope that hearing the story of the out-of-nowhere difficulties Stephanie and I faced will encourage anyone who might make a choice to seek greater meaning and more fulfillment, and then suddenly have to confront what feels like "opposition" to that choice. When we don't allow challenges to break us, we are usually stronger for having risen to meet them. And when we persevere, experiences that look like setbacks can turn out to be a prelude for good things to come.

I consider everything that happens to me as an evolutionary opportunity. It often feels as if I'm in a spiritual and emotional gymnasium, doing the work to become stronger. A place within us knows with certainty how the things that are unfolding can serve us in our personal and spiritual growth. Our invitation from life is to trust, graciously accepting the gifts that come and making the best of challenges when they arrive.

I believe we are always being guided to a better place. If we have faith and stay in our daily practice of prayer, meditation, and communing with nature, no matter what is happening around us, we will be able to remain aligned with the upward journey of our lives. Faith keeps us on track.

This journey of the soul takes us to grander and grander experiences and expressions of our true identity as *singularizations* or *individuations* of Divinity. The process will bring you more joy, satisfaction, and personal fulfillment than all the "worldly success" that money, fame, or power could ever provide.

I encourage you to embrace this dynamic fully by looking for the opportunity hidden within each crisis and trusting that you are on track.

# 41
# SPIRITUAL LEADERSHIP

I had shifted my focus from personal success to a different kind of fulfillment, and I did not let the many issues relating to my family's health and our home discourage me. As a result, the years 2008 and 2009 produced positive events for Humanity's Team. We were able to focus on spiritual leadership as well as publicly issue clear and powerful statements of belief and commitment.

I invite you to read the statements below to see if you agree with them and if they can be part of your own shift to an enlarged life purpose. But first, I'll share a little more about how they came into being.

In May of 2008, our Humanity's Team Global Council met in Buenos Aires, Argentina. During this meeting, a conversation arose that led to us make a spontaneous decision to create a document called a Declaration of Cultural Diversity. This statement continues to be of great importance to us to this day.

Each council member in attendance signed this declaration on May 21, 2008:

> "I commit to increasing my consciousness of cultural diversity, within my own country, as well as around the world, so that my Humanity's Team work and that of my teammates reflect this consciousness. This consciousness includes respect for cultural differences such as language, dress, and traditions; the ways societies organize themselves, their values, and religions; and the ways they interact with the environment."

We still consider this commitment an important part of the foundation of our Humanity's Team work. The declaration appears on our *Humanitysteam.org* website.

During the meeting, we also unanimously decided to give our second Humanity's Team spiritual leadership award to our meeting host, Country Coordinator Gabriel Avruj, for all he had done since he first joined Humanity's Team. Gabriel is an exemplary human being and a beautiful expression of Oneness and spiritual activism. We surprised him by presenting him with the award in front of his family and friends. It was the highlight of the week.

The following year, in April, 2009, Anna-Mari Pieterse, the country coordinator for South Africa, hosted our combined Global Council meeting and Spiritual Leadership award ceremony. Prior to these events, we had all voted to give Archbishop Desmond Tutu our third Spiritual Leadership award. The archbishop was a South African Anglican minister (he passed away in 2021) who believed in an unconditionally loving and omnipresent God, and he was deeply deserving of the award. He routinely condemned anti-gay, racist, and sexist governments in the region and throughout the world. He personally asked military-led regimes to end graft and oppressive practices in their countries. This was a dangerous thing to do at that time, but even threats to his life did not dissuade him from speaking out.

Archbishop Tutu also believed everything is an emanation of the Divine and was not afraid to say so. In his book *God Has A Dream*, Tutu shares, "You don't have to go around looking for God. You don't have to say 'Where is God?' Everyone around you—that is (part of) God." He was an ardent defender of universal suffrage, human rights, and non-violent protest. Tutu's advocacy and leadership contributed to the end of South African apartheid in 1993 and the installation of Nelson Mandela as the first black president of that country. In 1984, Tutu earned the Nobel Peace Prize for his efforts as a global peacemaker.

One of the reasons we chose Tutu for our Spiritual Leadership award was that his messages and his life were an embodiment of *Ubuntu*—the African expression of Oneness. He is considered one of the fathers of Ubuntu. At first, the conversations about Ubuntu focused on its humanistic aspects rather than its deeper spiritual connection to Divine love and essence, which is essential to its philosophy. Because of this, the Council agreed that we needed to highlight this aspect of Ubuntu in our own messaging.

To help facilitate this, Anna-Mari included this component in the video scripts she wrote for Archbishop Tutu to promote the event, and we also chose "Awaken the Spirit of Ubuntu" as the theme for the event.

Archbishop Tutu was well known for delighting audiences with his humor and giving memorable and inspiring speeches, and this night was no exception! The entire amphitheater was silent as he closed his acceptance speech with these words:

> "I encourage you to remember the magic of Who You Are. Live to your Highest Potential and see the potential in others. To celebrate the wonder of our diversity, and most importantly, to go and Be Who You Are."

We convened our Global Council meeting at the Protea Hotel by Marriott, which is just outside the gates of Kruger National Park—one of Africa's largest game reserves. During the meeting, we tackled how to create more public awareness of Oneness worldwide.

Among the questions we discussed:

- How could it be that so many prominent and upstanding leaders have talked about Oneness and the conscious journey, yet there is so little awareness among the population at large?
- If the global population remained unaware, was it even possible to create a sustainable and flourishing planet?

The answers to those questions were not optimistic, so we brainstormed ideas that might help.

We settled on the notion of modeling an initiative after the activism that led to the creation of "Earth Day." Earth Day, the brainchild of U.S. Senator Gaylord Nelson, was founded in 1970 as a day for the education and discussion of environmental issues. He hoped Earth Day would bring the environment to the national spotlight, which it did.

During our Global Council meeting, we decided our first step was to invite the United Nations to create a Global Oneness Day. Anna-Mari agreed to take the lead and work with me and a small team to create a "Oneness Declaration," which we planned to circulate until we'd gathered 50,000 signatures from people all over the world. Then we would include the declaration in our proposal to the United Nations.

Here is the declaration we created, in full:

### The Oneness Declaration

I declare that…

1. The idea that "We are all one—interrelated, interconnected, and interdependent with God, Life, and one another" is the spiritual message the world has been waiting for to bring about loving and sustainable answers to humanity's challenges.

2.  The world does not have to be the way it is, and individual people can change it, using the power of spiritual citizenship.

3.  Humanity is inherently good and has unlimited potential, and social transformation starts with personal transformation. I recognize the importance of connecting with my Divine Essence and inner wisdom throughout my life's journey, allowing the finest and the highest levels of human potential to flourish in me for the benefit of all.

4.  My aspirations will support the spiritual principles, global ethics, and universal values such as respect, justice, peace, dignity, freedom, responsibility, and cooperation that are the foundation of this declaration.

5.  Since human beings need one another to survive on this planet, I recognize that we are all in this together and that our larger community flourishes as we learn about one another and revel in the wonder and beauty of our diversities. I am doing my part in helping to bring about a culture in which the peoples of the world can address our common global concerns in a holistic, positive, and transformative way, and live together in peace.

6.  Since Oneness contains all of Life, including the things we perceive as being "other" than us, I realize that wholeness and togetherness can only be experienced through the recognition of the uniqueness, beauty, and purpose of all aspects of Life, and that this recognition starts with how I see my Self.

7.  I am part of the emerging consciousness that promotes a spirit of openness, inquiry, connection, and relationship with myself and the entire Universe, and continues to recognize the wonder, beauty, and mystery of it all.

8. I support the Global Oneness Summit, the annual event established for all of humanity to come together as one family, to discuss, celebrate, and experience Oneness with the Divine, one another, and all of Life.

9. The time for change is now and I am ready to be the change I want to see in the world.

Once we had drafted and discussed the declaration at length, there was great anticipation in the room. Country coordinators from Germany, the Netherlands, England, the United States, the Czech Republic, Argentina, France, and other countries were enthusiastic about launching our signature drive and then approaching the United Nations. We set up our Oneness Declaration on the Internet, so interested parties could easily read and sign it from anywhere in the world. The Internet allowed us to see the signature numbers jump in real time.

After we'd finished the last of our Global Council agenda items, we decided to devote our final day there to enjoying more of South Africa. We'd already gone out on wildlife-viewing expeditions; on this final day, half of us decided to enjoy the elephant rides that a vendor in the park was offering to tourists and the other half decided to go out on a final, big-game-viewing expedition.

I chose the expedition. It was everything I could have hoped for, as quite literally two of every species of big game in the area paraded in front of our open jeep during the drive, including species that are rarely seen in the park. We saw two elephants, two giraffes, two zebras, two lions, two cheetahs, two buffalo, two rhinos, two impala, and two species of eagle, and others. Gary Bailey, the master of ceremonies during the Freedom Park program and a board member of Humanity's Team South Africa, was with

141

us. As a native of the region, he'd been up close to these animals before—yet he was in complete disbelief that we saw them all on a single drive.

At one point, we all threw up our hands and said, "What's next?" half expecting we would round a stand of trees and run into Noah's Ark! To this day, I believe this whole experience was the Divine/God symbolically rewarding us for all we'd done over the previous week and all we were planning to do in the weeks and months ahead to bring the idea of Oneness further into the world.

I flew home to Colorado the following day with more than I could ever have hoped for—the unforgettable game drive, the personal time I'd gotten to spend with Archbishop Desmond Tutu, the wonderful memory of the award ceremony and his speech, all the amazing live music, and a Oneness Declaration that was going to help us awaken humanity.

Most importantly, I had a plan. I'd help collect 50,000 signatures and approach the United Nations to ask them to designate a Global Oneness Day.

Life was very good!

# 42
# THE ONENESS DECLARATION
# SIGNATURE DRIVE

The Oneness Declaration signature drive consumed the next twelve months. Our Global Council was on fire to reach our goal. Anna-Mari assumed a critical leadership role in gathering signatures and inspiring other country coordinators to do the same.

In the early days of the campaign, we'd see 50 to 100 signatures a week. By early 2010, we were seeing more than 1,000 signatures a week, including from small, remote countries such as Equatorial Guinea, Greenland, Guyana, the British Virgin Islands, the Republic of Djibouti, the Faroe Islands, Cook Islands, Gambia, Monaco, the Netherlands, the Antilles, Tunisia, and Togo.

Many key thought leaders were more than happy to support the drive by lending their name, signature, and photograph to the campaign. Desmond Tutu, Yoko Ono, Deepak Chopra, Marianne Williamson, Barbara Marx Hubbard—and of course, Neale Donald Walsch—and others agreed to personally back the campaign, which helped to raise its profile.

In the spring of 2010, it became obvious that we were going to exceed our 50,000-signature goal, so we wasted no time and reached out to the NGO (non-governmental organization) Committee on Spirituality, Values and Global Concerns at the United Nations in New York. Diane Williams was the chairperson at the time; after hearing the details of what we hoped to accomplish, she recommended we speak with Ambassador Anwarul K. Chowdhury—the former Undersecretary-General of the United Nations—because he had campaigned for good causes in the past and was active within the committee.

The committee arranged for us to meet the ambassador on the ground floor of the United Nations building in New York City in front of the Chagall Window at nine in the morning on May 20, 2010. We would be allowed to hold a brief ceremony as part of presenting our official proposal to him.

At final count, we had more than 52,000 signatures from 168 countries. We brought the Oneness Declaration, signatures, and other materials in a spiral binder. Diane Williams agreed to join us and voice her support for our initiative as part of the ceremony.

During the presentation, we shared our proposal with the ambassador and entreated the United Nations to begin a discussion about the Oneness

Declaration, and then to create a Global Oneness Day people could celebrate around the world.

Here is the summary we presented to the NGO Committee and to Ambassador Chowdhury:

> Humanity's Team sees a massive global fallacy as responsible for the world's crises, some of which have become so serious that they threaten to produce fundamental, abrupt, and decisive harm to the planet. The fallacy is the illusion of separation, which science increasingly shows is as false as the once-common fallacy that the Earth is flat.
>
> By contrast, Humanity's Team sees Oneness— recognizing we all share the planet equally as essential parts of a unified whole—as a truth that, when embraced, changes everything, creating workable "corrective actions" to break the causal chain responsible for the conflicts and discord stemming from the illusion.
>
> We find ourselves asking questions like this: Would the September 11, 2001 terrorist attacks have occurred if humanity recognized that we are all One? Would we tolerate accelerated global warming, extreme poverty and hunger, or gender inequality? Would we fight each other in the name of God?
>
> To us, the answer appeared obvious. The simple awareness that we are all One, and the creation of behavioral codes and international agreements reflecting this awareness, would shift the political, economic, social, and spiritual reality, and make possible unprecedented global cooperation.

This cooperation would lead by example to higher ethical standards, increased harmonizing and bridge-building, newfound dialogue and engagement, and market transparency and accountability. It would involve the provision of the necessities for a dignified life for all, including the vulnerable, with food, medicine, clean drinking water, and educational and health services, including for HIV/AIDS, malaria, and other diseases. It would also inspire international collaboration on other key Millennium Development Goals, such as advancing development, eradicating extreme poverty, protecting our common environment, and meeting the special needs of Africa, where the Humanity's Team Global Council held its April 2009, annual meeting.

After our presentation, Ambassador Chowdhury graciously thanked us for coming and spoke about the mission, vision, and purpose of the United Nations, including its focus on creating solidarity:

"I am most deeply touched by receiving this petition. This is a very unique effort dedicated to humanity and I congratulate Humanity's Team for making the effort to make this possible today with thousands of signatures. I believe that, as this simple ceremony is taking place in the most universal entity of the world, the United Nations, particularly in front of the meditation room, this ceremony becomes very significant. It has power, it has energy, it has dedication and commitment. So, I feel very proud that you have chosen to ask me to receive it on your behalf. And I believe that this is one of the proud moments for me, in my forty-five years of service, diplomatic service to the United Nations to my own country Bangladesh, and I believe that you have decided to give it to a person who along with all of my colleagues here and I am so proud that they are joining us here to work, to advance, to build the culture of peace in this world. The culture of peace has eight areas of action and one of them is dedicated to tolerance, understanding, and solidarity, all these must be promoted to achieve Oneness. Oneness...feeling a sense of Oneness for Mother Earth, for humanity, for each one of us is essential to make this world a better place. I believe that until there is a sense of solidarity among the peoples of the world, all our efforts for peace and security will go nowhere."

He agreed that Global Oneness Day could be an important catalyst for change—but he said it would take too long for the United Nations to initiate discussion on the idea and come to consensus. Instead, he encouraged us to create Global Oneness Day ourselves.

## 43
# THE FIRST GLOBAL ONENESS DAY

Events in my life repeatedly have made it clear to me that, when it looks on the surface like a mission has not been accomplished, I've really just taken the first step toward accomplishing even more.

Ambassador Chowdhury's observation and suggestion could have been discouraging at the time, but instead, they served to spur us on, inspiring us to move forward with determination just eight weeks later when, in July of 2010, the Humanity's Team Global Council met virtually to discuss his recommendation. We decided to create Global Oneness Day on October 24, which is also United Nations Day.

We chose to do this because United Nations Day and Global Oneness Day share common visions for a compassionate and sustainable world, and the U.N. Millennium Goals very much align with what Global Oneness Day is about. We agreed there could be a powerful synergy created if these two days of activism occurred on a common day.

We celebrated the first Global Oneness Day twelve weeks later, on October 24, 2010 with a simple conference call. The meeting line to which we had access could only accommodate 1,000 people, and it was full. Key leaders like Neale Donald Walsch, Barbara Marx Hubbard, and others joined us and spoke to those who had gathered on the call about our present world and why raising awareness of Oneness and celebrating it was so critical to our future. Others around the globe celebrated with community events, drum circles, service programs, and performances planned by our wonderful and committed country coordinators.

A year later, for Global Oneness Day 2011, we took part in an in-person public event in Fort Collins, Colorado, with musicians and other entertainers, all focusing on the power of Oneness. Events also took place in Canada, England, France, Portugal, Argentina, Columbia, South Africa, and other countries.

Not satisfied to rest on these gratifying accomplishments, we took the next step and created an all-day online program for Global Oneness Day that kicked off with a live-streamed celebration in Australia and then followed the sun's path around the globe. Humanity's Team, The Association for Global New Thought (AGNT), and The Shift Network co-promoted the program. We drew in tens of thousands of people. This has evolved into a weeklong, worldwide, annual online event that is in its thirteenth year at the time of this writing.

I've shared this story with you here in hopes that it will inspire you to never give up on things you really want to do, even if your first attempts don't bear the fruit you'd hoped.

Along with the expansion of Global Oneness Day, the presentation of our Spiritual Leadership award also became more public and important as we drew attention to the courageous actions of spiritual leaders globally who embodied Oneness as an inner and outer quality, each in their own authentic and powerful way. I hope you'll be as inspired as our whole support team has been as you read about the choices, decisions, and actions in service to others of the two recipients noted here.

In 2010, we presented the award to Andrew Harvey, a British author, religious scholar, and teacher of mystic traditions, at a ceremony in New York City following our meeting at the United Nations. Harvey's website encourages people to join in what he calls "Sacred Activism," a form of service to humanity. He describes his work this way:

> "Andrew Harvey is the Founder and Director of the Institute of Sacred Activism, an international organization focused on inviting concerned people to take up the challenge of our contemporary global crisis by becoming inspired, effective, and practical agents of institutional and systemic change, in order to create peace and sustainability. Sacred Activism is a transforming force of compassion-in-action that is born of a fusion of deep spiritual knowledge, courage, love, and passion, with wise radical action in the world. The large-scale practice of Sacred Activism can become an essential force for preserving and healing the planet and its inhabitants..."

Whenever people asked Andrew what call to Sacred Activism they should take up, Andrew would say, "In the middle of the night, when you awaken, what breaks your heart about the world we live in? What cause are you most passionate about? Serve that."

In 2011, we presented the award to Immaculee Ilibagiza. The ceremony was conducted as a virtual Skype event because our Global Council meeting was in Delphi, Greece, while Immaculee was at her home in New York at the time.

Immaculee survived the 1994 Rwandan genocide by hiding for ninety-one days, with seven other women, in a small bathroom no larger than three-by-four feet that was concealed behind a wardrobe in the home of a Hutu pastor. During the genocide, men, women, and children were indiscriminately slaughtered. Angry townspeople repeatedly entered the home and came dangerously close to finding Immaculee and others hiding there.

Her website shares this additional information:

> "During the genocide, all of Ilibagiza's family were killed, except for one brother who was out of the country at the time. In her book, *Left to Tell: Discovering God Amidst the Rwandan Holocaust* (2006), Ilibagiza shares how her Catholic faith guided her through her ordeal and describes her eventual forgiveness and compassion toward her family's killers. Today, Immaculee is regarded as one of the world's leading speakers on faith, hope and forgiveness. She has shared this universal message with world leaders, school children, multinational corporations, churches, and at events and conferences around the world."

We vowed to continue to give the award whenever we identified an individual who embodied Oneness in their lives, spreading the messages of unity in their own way, and making an important contribution in the world.

## 44
# COMING TOGETHER AS ONE FOR THE NEXT STAGE OF GROWTH

The 2011 meeting in Delphi, Greece was our largest yet, with nearly forty Global Council leaders attending. We had decided that this year, we would truly become an "active and coordinated movement."

Over the previous years, we'd taken steps in this direction by working together to create our world tour, the Oneness Declaration, and Global Oneness Day—but our activity was still decentralized rather than coordinated.

We hadn't yet reached the stage where we could function as a cohesive team, with each member working in unison with others around the world.

At this point, we were all still volunteers. Financial donations had been scarce, and we had not yet discovered a way to monetize our educational outreach. This created hardship for our support team and their families. I could feel their concern whenever I was with them.

Some Global Council members suggested we adjust our course and "mainstream" ourselves. One felt we should refocus on Oneness as something *humanistic*. Some scientists contend that we are one modern, human family that evolved from the original people of Africa.

Another member felt we should create education programs based on the popular movie, *The Secret.* The public seemed fascinated with the process of creating vision boards to manifest prosperity.

Charting a course was easier because, in our earlier work, we had anchored Humanity's Team in "end statements" that reflected our core mission. Humanity's Team would always stand for a new spirituality, through which we would try to live our lives in friendship and communion with the Divine, the Earth, and life, while each of us also sought to grow into our highest aspiration and possibility.

During the meeting in Greece, we reaffirmed that vision and the overall mission that had brought us together in 2003 for the original Humanity's Team launch. We chose to expand our range of activities and we renewed our commitment to awaken humanity to Oneness in a generation.

We were well aware of how bold this commitment was, but we believed the Divine was guiding us—and in the Divine, all things are possible. We asked ourselves questions like, "What happens if there is no planetary awakening to conscious living in this generation? What if there is no flourishing? What happens if we stay stuck in a 'separation state' of consciousness?"

The answers were apparent. Humanity and the Earth had no time to lose.

Our last action was to create this Oneness Statement: "Oneness is the energy of love that lies within and connects all of life, enabling us to recognize ourselves in everything. The universe is one being, and we are its cells, all essential and responsible for the well-being of the whole."

The meeting led to pivotal shifts at Humanity's Team. Our strategic plan had tightened everything up, and our mission was no longer just to support diverse voices; now, it was about executing a specific plan together, as one. Each of us had work to do, every day, toward that goal.

Many of the key leaders who had collaborated closely with us for almost a decade decided to step back from their direct involvement. They were pioneers who had helped create the foundation for the future we were now building toward. Each of them had contributed substantial time and resources to what the organization had become—but many needed to get back to earning a steady income, and we still didn't have enough money coming in to pay salaries. While they pledged their moral support for our continuing mission, they would not be involved in the day-to-day planning and execution of our new agendas.

## 45
# A COORDINATED AND HARMONIOUS TEAM

Upon returning home, our focus was to create a coordinated, harmonious, and effective support team so we could get important things done.

At that time, each team member was still operating from a home-office space. They did so at their own expense, without income or even reimbursement, aside from the little bit of scholarship we'd created for attending Global Council meetings. But we were committed to driving a plan that would further our reach and impact as well as create sustainable income for all those in mission-critical roles. Our members needed to be compensated for their time, to help maintain their livelihood.

Dee Meyer, who had attended the meeting in Greece, was an essential and irreplaceable business associate during this period. She later became our Worldwide Operations Director.

When I'd first met Dee, she owned a landscape design firm and was volunteering for a non-profit based in Boulder called The Caritas Spiritual Center, which focused on teaching people how to become conduits for God's love and light. The center hosted programs with spiritual authors who came through town. She later said something just "clicked" for her when she learned about the work Humanity's Team was doing. She closed her business and left Caritas to make herself more available to us. Initially, she focused on children's education programs, but before long, she took on additional responsibilities.

I'm telling you a little of Dee's story because it illustrates crucial elements of the conscious journey, which is about engaging in a spiritual practice that supports our inner "being state." This practice involves setting aside time to commune with the Divine and Nature. Through this process, we become more patient, more gentle, more compassionate, more loving, and more devoted to service.

Dee set aside this kind of time in her life. I consider her a living expression of what it means to be *conscious*. She would always say "yes" to helping the team. She did whatever she could to empower our agenda of planetary awakening and flourishing at every level of life—in our home, our community, our country, and in the larger world.

Dee never engaged in any "us versus them" perspectives because she was determined to help people on the team work together in harmony, honor, and respect. She is now the center of our Humanity's Team operations on a global level.

Upon our return from Greece, we began to focus on transformational education— but unfortunately, our initial program was not successful. The practice of *mindfulness* was attracting attention in the world, but our instructor wasn't well known and we weren't yet trained in the process of

153

marketing and supporting online education. We created something we called Humanity's Team University, but it never took off.

We also tried to monetize our work by creating "upgrade" packages for recordings and transcripts and by soliciting donations from those who resonated with our message and vision. This generated just a small amount of revenue; without more funding, our resources to move the organization to the next level were limited.

But life often has surprises in store for us. Exciting developments lay just ahead.

## 46
# BARBARA MARX HUBBARD AND THE TWELVE SPHERES OF LIFE

In 2012, Humanity's Team launched an important initiative called "Oneness in the Twelve Spheres of Life."

This program was born from the awareness that Oneness is something with important applications in our day-to-day lives. We wanted to consider what the future might look like if we explored our Oneness in the context of each of the twelve spheres of life detailed below.

If all of life is connected at a deep level, and if our basic nature is that of the Divine, then love must be at the core of life experiences. But how could we create new forms of education in the world that showed what this means? How would it affect our relationships with others? Does this mean we need to re-imagine healthcare—and if so, how would this work?

We hoped the answers to these questions might illuminate what our world would look like once we, as a species, awaken to our true nature.

We decided to partner with our friend, bestselling author and spiritual teacher Barbara Marx Hubbard, to create the program. She had developed something she called "The Wheel of Co-Creation"—also called the "12 around 1" model—where each sector represents part of society and part of the nature of the cosmos. The twelve societal sectors represent the basic functions of any community.

The Wheel of Co-Creation is a powerful look at a whole-systems shift as we evolve from *Homo sapiens* to what Barbara called "*Homo Universalis*" (our future, more enlightened selves). The model shows the substantial transformation that every sector of society will undergo to reach this state. The Wheel can help the natural re-patterning of society to a more harmonious order.

The Wheel of Co-Creation is also a tool for our inner journey, attuning us to what renowned Hungarian philosopher Ervin Laszlo describes as "the rhythms and balances of nature." It also can help foster the joyful rhythm and balance that are possible in social interaction. We activate the Wheel of Co-Creation and turn on the spiral from the inside out. In this way, the wheel emulates how life works.

The saying, "As within, so without," means that when something new emerges from within, it is expressed in the outer world. This is true in both our individual experience and our collective experience. As we feel more loving, more patient, and more kind, we express this when reaching out to others—and because they can *feel* this, our relationships change.

As we become more heart-centered, we create more healthy and harmonious structures around us. Barbara said this kind of "social synergy" always leads to greater public good. In her own words:

"It is important to remember that in the Wheel, we are fostering a more co-creative society and a more participatory, synergistic democracy, not by revolution, but by evolutionary action. The Wheel facilitates creating programs and connecting initiatives that point to holistic grassroots processes and facilitates synergy where we seek common goals and match needs and resources throughout the whole system, rather than remain isolated in pursuits that are not connected. From the point of view of evolution, the Wheel represents a vital step forward toward a cooperative world.

"When the Wheel of Co-Creation is fully activated, we see the new world that is already arising in our midst. It offers us a coherent picture of humanity, as well as our whole planetary system as a living organism. It will tell us where the problems are, who is working to solve them, and where we can find the needed innovations—all organic elements of a living, holistic system of relationships. It will provide us with 'the news of who we are becoming' and inspire us to keep moving forward so we may come into our true potential and destiny."

The Twelve Spheres are representative of the basic functions and activities of any community and are all interconnected. They are presented in alphabetical order, using a continuous range of spectral colors.

1. ARTS
2. ECONOMICS
3. EDUCATION
4. ENVIRONMENT
5. GOVERNANCE
6. HEALTH
7. INFRASTRUCTURE
8. JUSTICE
9. MEDIA

10. RELATIONS
11. SCIENCE
12. SPIRITUALITY

We can look to the Wheel of Co-Creation for vision, perspective, and guidance as we move ahead into the future. Using this wheel as a model, we might look into the future and see things like...

- Hospitals placing an emphasis on effectiveness (real love and connection) over efficiency (taking a patient's temperature and then moving on).
- Businesses with cultures attuned to the rhythms and balances of nature, in service to communities and the world and not exclusively bound to the priority of financial profit.
- Education systems supporting the whole child's growth and development rather than just academic achievement.
- Relationships with family, friends, and coworkers based on a deep and abiding love, rather than codependent and transactional (I'll give you this if you give me that) relationships.
- A focus on that which is life-sustaining, life-supporting, and life-enhancing when we consider the Earth and all of life on the planet.

Coming into 2013, we were eager to identify a worthy candidate for our Humanity's Team Spiritual Leadership award. After considering deserving leaders, we unanimously settled on Barbara.

Barbara had been born into a wealthy family in 1929. Her father's company, Marx Toys, was one of the most well-known toy companies in the world at that time, and her father's high profile gave her access to global leaders as she was growing up. This made a deep impression upon young Barbara. She was invited to the White House to meet President Eisenhower; during that meeting, she asked the president: "What is the meaning of our power that is good?"

President Eisenhower was reported to have said, "I haven't the slightest idea."

Barbara responded, "Well, we'll have to find out, won't we?"

She began to do exactly that, pursuing her own inquiry into the human experience and becoming a pioneer in the human-potential movement. In the 1970s, she began attending and eventually speaking at futurist conferences to share her findings.

As an adult, she felt compelled to walk away from her family's life of privilege so she could focus on her research full time and do everything she could to help create a more just and progressive society. She soon began creating her own conferences and organizations—including the Committee for the Future, Women of Vision in Action, and The Alliance for the Advancement of Conscious Evolution—to expand and enlist others in exploring the discoveries she was making.

Her public presence brought her into such prominence that in 1984, she became the first woman to have her name entered into consideration for the vice-presidency of the United States on the Democratic ticket with Walter Mondale. While Mondale eventually chose Geraldine Ferraro as his running mate, Barbara gave a speech at the Democratic convention that year, which further elevated her stature worldwide.

In 1998, she published her first book, *Conscious Evolution: Awakening the Power of Our Social Potential,* and became one of America's preeminent evolutionary thinkers and public speakers.

Barbara's lifelong inquiry and the answers she found formed the basis for the body of work that would define her life. She believed that our current planetary crisis is actually a birth. She often said that we are in a moment of decision where we must choose between regression (an inability to solve our world's problems) and conscious evolution (taking control of our destiny and making wise choices about how we live with each other and the Earth).

She believed global change happens when we work tirelessly and collectively for the greater good, and that despite our many challenges, the world is on the threshold of great possibility: our own conscious evolution, which will lead to the birth of a New Humanity.

Humanity's Team presented Barbara with our Spiritual Leadership Award at Sunrise Ranch in Loveland, Colorado, on May 27, 2013.

# 47
# TRAGEDY STRIKES ONE OF OUR OWN

During the fall of 2013, in the middle of all our work, the Humanity's Team community faced a test. The skies in Colorado opened up, dropping more than seventeen inches of rain over eight days. This would become known as a "thousand-year" rain. It was followed by a historic flood. More than 550 homes were damaged; more than a thousand people had to be evacuated by air.

When the storm finally cleared, eight people had died and six were missing. Colorado suffered more than a billion dollars in property damage.

Our Humanity's Team operations director, Dee Meyer, who I mentioned in a previous chapter, lived in a lovely, rented home in the city of Jamestown, about twelve miles northwest of Boulder. The town nestles in the Rocky Mountains with the James Creek flowing through its center. After the massive rains of 2013, the James Creek overflowed its banks and inundated the tiny town, carrying away homes. The flood triggered catastrophic landslides; the fire station and other parts of the community were buried under thousands of tons of mud.

Dee's home stood high on the south bank of James Creek. A neighbor pounded on her door at three a.m. to warn her and her family to evacuate immediately. They grabbed their dogs and rushed to a shelter with just the clothes they were wearing.

Hours later, Dee and her family walked back as close as they dared and watched as her house tumbled into James Creek and disintegrated in a matter of minutes. She could only stand by helplessly while their precious personal belongings floated downstream. They lost everything.

Dee and her family were among those airlifted out of Jamestown. Her renter's insurance did not include flood protection, so she was financially devastated and had nowhere to turn.

Our Humanity's Team community was heartbroken about this news. We invited those who could afford to donate a little to help Dee and her family. Checks poured in, ranging from five dollars to hundreds of dollars, and our leadership team contributed a substantial amount, as well. We were able to give Dee enough financial support to replace what she had lost and get on her feet again.

This tragedy ended as well as it could have, once again proving the power of honoring our Oneness by helping others in their times of need.

# 48
# NELSON MANDELA AND THE MESSAGE OF "WE NOT ME"

In December 2013, Nelson Mandela, the great leader based in South Africa, passed away. The world was sad to see him go but grateful for the inspiring life he had lived.

Kofi Annan, the former United Nations Secretary General, said Mandela was "perhaps the most respected, most admired international figure in the world." Not since Gandhi had the world known a man such as this. When he walked into a room, people would slip into hushed silence so they could watch him without distraction.

I think most people were aware that the South African government had unjustly imprisoned Mandela. He spent twenty-seven years isolated on Robben Island before public pressure forced his release. Mandela was without freedom for a good part of his life. His extended incarceration also cost him his marriage.

While Mandela's personal sacrifice was great, his commitment to humanity led to substantial accomplishments. He and Archbishop Desmond Tutu, who I discussed earlier, brought the South African spiritual tradition of Ubuntu to the world's attention. South Africans felt that Mandela, like Tutu, embodied Ubuntu; Mandela used the concept to lead their country to a peaceful, post-apartheid transition.

Beginning in the mid-1990s, largely as the result of the work of Mandela and Tutu, Ubuntu defined South African society, and its meaning and impact began to spill over to other parts of the world.

President Barack Obama once said, "Mandela understood the ties that bind the human spirit. There is a word in South Africa—Ubuntu—that describes his greatest gift—his recognition that we are all bound together

161

in ways that can be invisible to the eye, that there is a Oneness of humanity, that we achieve ourselves by sharing ourselves with others, and caring for all those around us."

The life and legacy of Nelson Mandela deeply moved all of us at Humanity's Team. Our Global Council reached out to his family and foundation to let them know we intended to posthumously give him our 2014 Spiritual Leadership Award. Anna-Mari Pieterse, our South African country coordinator, extended the invitation and also handled all of the arrangements to prepare for the ceremony in July of 2014.

Our Humanity's Team Global Council journeyed to South Africa and celebrated Mandela's life and achievement through two exciting public events. The first event, the "Ubuntu Indaba: A Spiritual Witnessing and Celebration of the Life of the Late Mr. Nelson Mandela" was held at the Nelson Mandela Centre, where Mandela worked during the later years of life. While people often spoke of Nelson Mandela and Ubuntu in the same sentence, as far as I know, this was the first event that had been arranged specifically to reflect on his Ubuntu qualities, contributions, and legacy to South Africa.

The second event was the following day at Freedom Park in Pretoria, where we had held the 2009 event. We called it "Walk for an Ubuntu Conscious South Africa – I Am Because We Are." The Nelson Mandela Foundation accepted our Spiritual Leadership Award on Mandela's behalf. A memorable and exciting feature of the event was the attendance of leaders of the first people of Africa, the KhoiSan.

Before the program began, I had an opportunity to sit privately with George Bizos, Mandela's lifelong friend and lawyer, who had visited him throughout the prison years. Bizos talked to me about Mandela's compassion and said Mandela had invited guards from the prison where he'd been confined to be part of his inauguration swearing-in ceremony.

Bizos also told me that when people reached out to Mandela following his presidency, asking how they might help him, Mandela was always quick to invite financial contribution to a school, a hospital, or a project that would benefit South Africa as a whole or local communities. He never solicited funds for himself or his family. He always drew attention to his team, including his partners and colleagues, instead of himself.

As Bizos explained: "He was always about 'We' and not 'Me.'"

## 49
# HUMANITY'S TEAM CORE VALUES

Following the programs with the Mandela Foundation, we were off to our Global Council meeting at the Kruger Park gate, about 230 miles north of Johannesburg, where we'd also held a gathering five years earlier.

During this session, we started work on our Humanity's Team Core Values statements. Over the years, we had amassed an archive of more than 500 inspiring and informative interviews with thought leaders of the conscious evolution movement. We began to develop an idea called Community Circle to make the interviews available to anyone interested in listening to and watching them.

We were eleven years in, following our launch in 2003, and things were going smoothly. As a next step, we decided this was the time to become more clear about our worldwide culture, so we could attract people who were a good fit with our growing team.

To help us better understand what was working within our organization and which of our characteristics defined us, we interviewed each other. We asked questions like: What is our culture? How does it work? How can our colleagues and partners contribute to our work in the world? What do we seek in new recruits?

We evaluated these interviews over the months that followed and slowly began to craft a series of statements defining what it meant to be a member of Humanity's Team. Eighteen months of fine-tuning later, we finally felt it was ready to share with the world.

### Humanity's Team Core Values

To the best of our ability, we will…

1. Courageously serve the big agenda: awakening ourselves and the world to Oneness.
2. Be humble and embody the spirit of "servant leadership."
3. Commit to personal transformation: education, daily inner practice, and personal growth.
4. Live life as One with the Divine and all of life (follow the 5 Steps to Peace).
5. Co-create with Humanity's Team colleagues by deeply listening for inner guidance and feeling what is seeking to emerge.
6. Have clear intentions, take the initiative, and be willing to take on additional responsibilities if teammates struggle to fulfill their commitments.
7. Build a positive team through love, honesty, trust, communication, support, harmony, respect, and fun in all relationships.
8. Do more with less, and trust that the Divine provides us with all we need to fulfill our clear, purposeful intentions.
9. Invite, inspire, involve, and mentor those who want to live as One and contribute to Humanity's Team.

10. And, if ever our ideas don't align with the leadership team's consensus, we agree to accept the decision and support it in the spirit of Oneness, or gracefully resign.

Number 10 may seem like a strange addition to the list, but it is a best practice in well-run organizations to invite people to evaluate important decisions and determine whether they should support decisions they don't necessarily like.

There is no reason to remain on a team when you fall out of vision alignment with those in the majority. This core value is an escape hatch for those who truly cannot live with a decision that is counter to something about which they have strong feelings. It's better to let someone go and be thankful for their contributions than to have them stay and end up with what Abraham Lincoln described when he said, "A house divided against itself cannot stand."

At this point in Humanity's Team's growth, we still didn't have enough funding. We continued to look for new ways to monetize the good work we were doing. The Community Circle project looked promising, because it could both support continuing education and provide a modest income stream. It might generate enough money to let us offer stipends and salaries for those who were part of our small but mission-critical staff.

For a nominal monthly fee, members of the public could gain access to our wealth of audio and video interviews anytime they wanted, 24/7. We felt that these inspiring interviews would help people in our community accelerate their conscious journeys. Excited about the possibilities, we agreed to move forward with launch plans.

## 50
# THE CONSCIOUS BUSINESS MOVEMENT

About this time, the director for Green Technologies at Intel, John Thomas, called to ask me about the possibility of coming to work for Humanity's Team. He brought to my attention a program created by Social Venture Partners and Encore, which paid a small salary to business leaders who took "assignments" in non-profit organizations. He asked if I might apply for these funds so I could bring him on board at Humanity's Team at no cost to us.

I looked into the program and applied for the funding, which was quickly approved. John officially joined the team to assist us in whatever way he could. Though the original agreement with John was for two years, he ended up staying with us for three, making valuable contributions to our success before he moved on to other things.

Only a few months into John's time with us, he and I decided that Humanity's Team should make it one of our primary areas of focus to help businesses become more conscious in their practices.

The business community is in the driver's seat of both the economy and our culture. Bringing that community into more conscious behavior is a foundational necessity. Conscious businesses can create the urgent change needed to reverse the incredibly destructive effects that conventional businesses have wreaked upon our world.

Our global economy has been addicted to growth at any cost along with unbridled capitalism. The frequent industrial environmental disasters are examples of the damage companies do to the natural world.

While John and I knew that focusing on catalyzing changes in the business world was critical, we also knew that this alone wasn't going to be enough. We agreed that a reductive and analytical way of doing business has caused the world's challenges and upheaval.

So many have exploited life for perceived human betterment. Many of us have not lived as if life is sacred. We have been willing to harm each other and the planet. This degenerative way of living has impoverished our sense of the interconnectedness of all things. This in turn has created disharmony, stress, social and ecological degradation, and large-scale breakdown in many aspects of life.

The root cause is our sense of separateness. We have become disconnected from nature and each other. Only reconnection can integrate our inner-outer life dynamic once again. This requires a shift in consciousness. We must prioritize that which is life-affirming and nurture Earth's ecosystems.

It was obvious to us that, before there could be a true revolution in business, we needed a revolution in humanity's consciousness.

In 2014, Humanity's Team began studying progressive business models such as B Corps, Benefit Corps, and Conscious Capitalism to help us understand what role we might play in curbing business abuse. These models were designed as templates for creating conscious business systems that support a flourishing world. One defining aspect of B Corps is their focus on the 3Ps of business: people, planet, and profit.

We determined that while those business models were valuable and pointed businesses in more healthy directions, they didn't go far enough. They ignored the concept of creating truly conscious businesses and even stopped short of defining "conscious business" in a manner that people could manifest worldwide.

When there is no focus on inner transformation, it's easy to simply swap out a CEO and create a new company direction with no regard for its impact on others. It is our inner transformation that defines and anchors us.

When we embrace our deeply held values, we feel connected to our creator, nature, life, and community. The culture of a company can become a container for this heartfelt way of being. All collaboration and decision-making occur within this container.

Looking out at the world, the organization sees a deeply interconnected experience. No longer do we view the world in a Newtonian way, where things may be broken into discrete parts. We see the ecology of life; we see holistically. This kind of organization can be a catalyst for healthy communities and a healthy world.

# 51
# THE '4-P' MODEL: PEOPLE, PLANET, PRESENCE, AND PROFIT

In the area of business, outer transformation means people, planet, and profit. This means that businesses focus on the welfare of people and planet, not just their shareholder's profit margin.

But inner transformation is also critically important if we are to bring true flourishing to business and to the planet. Inner transformation focuses on practices like mindfulness, but it also goes beyond to a deeper place where we commune with our source. People have discovered valid and compelling channels to commune with this source, ranging from practicing spiritual techniques to studying quantum physics. Each of these begins with a firm foundational belief in the Divine.

We had planted the seeds for this shift at Humanity's Team during Global Oneness Day back in 2011, where we began referring to a "4-P" model: people, planet, *presence*, and profit. We felt that adding *presence* to the mix would provide the missing ingredient for creating wholeness, unity, and awakened consciousness.

By "presence," we mean a way of looking out at the world and being present to its deeply spiritual, interconnected ecology. When we consider the world in this way, everything changes. We begin to see the likeness and image of God in ourselves, each other, and the world around us. There are people who experience a resonant connection with our source in less spiritual terms, perhaps as an unambiguous, uplifting energy that threads through all things, connecting all life forms.

While business models that focus only on outer transformation can, of course, help businesses do less harm, a truly flourishing business is also a product of inner transformation. When individuals within the organization fully embrace the experience of serving love, beauty, goodness, and truth, it affects the work they do in all kinds of positive ways.

Presence shapes both how we see ourselves and what we see when we look out on the world. It is critical that we become anchored in this new perspective on reality, so we can remember how sacred life is and live in service to it.

It's only a matter of time before this perspective finds its way into the workplace. The practice of mindfulness is already becoming popular. The great religions of the world honor Divine inspiration and connection with Source; even science is increasingly confirming that all the cosmos are intimately connected, making us part of a natural, social web of life that nurtures and sustains us.

Since spirituality, religion, and leading scientific thought all support a focus on inner transformation, if the core values and culture of a company are open and inclusive—honoring diverse spiritual, religious, and scientific perspectives—that company will be set up for greater success on every level.

Engaging in conscious business creates the opportunity for integration of our deeply held values. Conventional businesses focus exclusively—and often blindly—on financial gain. This has created the social and economic quagmire we stand in today. A conscious business decides how it can meaningfully contribute first and *then* focuses on financial gain.

Michael Bernard Beckwith, the founding minister and spiritual director at the Agape International Spiritual Center in Beverly Hills, California, has shared that a conscious business is a mission with a business—not a business with a mission.

Ken Wilber, an American philosopher and writer on transpersonal psychology, has written that too much focus on the outer world creates a kind of "flatland," where consciousness is caught in a mundane experience of routines and dullness that doesn't nourish or inspire the whole person or organization.

Overcoming this problem is one of the biggest challenges in the world today.

# 52
# THE CREATION OF THE CONSCIOUS BUSINESS ALLIANCE

The enormity of this task—introducing Oneness consciousness to businesses—inspired both John Thomas and me. We developed a plan we hoped would support a shift toward conscious business on a global scale.

Our initial step involved reaching out to three of our NGO (non-governmental organization) partners about teaming up to create a Conscious Business Declaration like our Global Oneness Declaration.

We contacted Ervin Laszlo at The Club of Budapest; Hiroo Saionji, Founder of the Goi Peace Foundation; and Chris Laszlo (Ervin's son) from the Fowler Center for Business, where he works as an Agent for Public Benefit at Case Western Reserve University. In 2014, they all agreed to work with Humanity's Team to develop a Conscious Business Declaration and move the agenda forward.

We set out to create a brief, yet comprehensive, list of statements that businesses could use to help them stay on track in adopting and maintaining more conscious practices in their day-to-day operations. We also wanted to describe the role conscious businesses can play in creating a flourishing world, so the leaders of these businesses could easily grasp this concept and conform business models across intercontinental operations.

We spent a little over a year fine-tuning the declaration before we decided it was ready for release. In this declaration, we use "business" to mean the whole body of all commerce and the individual elements thereof.

Here's the preamble:

As part of a global community, we are committed to developing the awareness and skills needed to consciously evolve our organizations in alignment with these principles:

1.  We Are One with humanity and all of life. Business and all institutions of the human community are integral parts of a single reality—interrelated, interconnected, and interdependent.

2. In line with this reality, the purpose of Business is to increase economic prosperity while contributing to a healthy environment and improving human well-being.

3. Business must go beyond sustainability and the philosophy of "do no harm" to restoring the self-renewing integrity of the Earth.

4. Business must operate with economic, social, and ecological transparency.

5. Business must behave as a positive and proactive member of the local and global communities in which it operates.

6. Business that sees, honors, and celebrates the essential inter-connected nature of all human beings and all life maximizes human potential and helps create a world that works for all.

7. When aligned with these principles, Business is the most powerful engine on Earth for creating prosperity and flourishing for all.

These principles also work as catalysts to inspire us as individuals to align with the actions of conscious evolution. I encourage you to try replacing the word "business" with the word "I" and see how each of these statements feels to you. Consider them as the basis for action steps in the world.

If you work in the business world, I invite you to envision how these might apply to every action you take in your job responsibilities. If you resonate with the declaration, whether on a personal or professional level, I invite you to add your name in solidarity by signing it at *ConsciousBusinessDeclaration.org.*

John and I discussed how we could better encourage others to adopt conscious business practices and what those next steps for Humanity's Team would look like. Once the declaration was complete, we began developing a training program to help businesses at all levels to initiate and then live up to the declaration's statements.

Using a structured program, we would teach people how to become Conscious Business Change Agents (CBCA). They could apply the skills they learned in the program to launch a conscious business or transform any existing business into one with a conscious framework.

We launched the CBCA training program in 2016. In the years since then, others have made positive contributions to its evolution.

# 53
# A FIRST FOR THE SPIRITUAL LEADERSHIP AWARD

In 2015, the year prior to creating the CBCA program, we chose, for the first time, to give our Spiritual Leadership Award to two people: renowned spiritual leader Michael Bernard Beckwith and his wife at the time, Rickie Byars (Beckwith).

Michael and Rickie, both on their own and in partnership, were making a tremendous impact globally. Since the purpose of the award is to honor those who promote and accelerate the conscious journey, helping our species to progress and evolve, we felt it was time to acknowledge their dedication and accomplishments.

As the saying goes, "God does not call the qualified; God qualifies those who are called." Michael said this was certainly true for him (and it has been true for so many others in the transformational education community, including me).

Michael had been a medical student at the University of Southern California when events conspired to alter the course of his life. He became inspired to go into spiritual ministry. Shortly after completing his ministry in education with the Centers for Spiritual Living, he founded the Agape International Spiritual Center in Southern California.

He also then cofounded the Association for Global New Thought and the Season for Nonviolence; both groups have touched millions of people around the world and served as umbrella organizations for nurturing spiritual practices and community outreach. Over the years that followed, the Agape International Spiritual Center has grown into one of the largest New Thought/Ancient Wisdom communities in the world.

Rickie is an acclaimed and beloved singer-songwriter in the genre of inspirational, New Thought music. She joined the Agape Center as the director of the soon-to-be-world-renowned Agape International Choir, and when she and Michael eventually married, they became a powerhouse team, inspiring others around the globe through their media appearances, TEDx talks, and the weekly services, broadcast to the world, during which they both shared their gifts and talents.

The evening before the award ceremony, we gathered with Michael and Rickie at Peaceful Valley Ranch, just outside Boulder, where we talked and shared our personal stories about the individual journeys that led us to where we were.

We then traveled to Sunrise Ranch in Loveland the next day for the award ceremony, where Michael spoke about his process for creating inner peace and awakened awareness in our everyday lives. He called on all those present to model this way of living together, so that it might spread everywhere.

Rickie performed deeply uplifting songs that had everyone in attendance standing and singing along.

# 54
# A THEORY OF EVERYTHING

In early 2016, we began discussing our next Spiritual Leadership Award recipient. Since we'd focused on the heart and inspiration in 2015 with Michael Beckwith and Rickie Byars, we decided to focus on human knowledge and philosophy for the 2016 award. Renowned philosopher Ken Wilber was our unanimous choice.

Ken had developed something he called Integral Theory, a systemic philosophy which suggests the synthesis of all human knowledge and experience. Its basic framework is a stunningly simple but comprehensive approach to reality called "all quadrants, all levels, all lines, all states, all types"—AQAL for short.

In his own words, "These five crucial elements represent the fewest possible factors required to create the fullest possible understanding of the universe—from the Big Bang, to the evolution of life, to the astonishing breadth of human thought and human development."

The left side of his model is devoted to interior states of development; the right side represents exterior states. The upper quadrants focus on individual states, and the lower quadrants focus on collective states. Wikipedia describes it this way: "It is a comprehensive approach to reality, a metatheory that attempts to explain how academic disciplines and every form of knowledge and experience fit together coherently."

In short, Wilber says, "It is a theory of everything."

Using the AQAL approach, Wilber makes observations about reality, including the fact that we effectively live in the "flatland" I mentioned earlier, where interior quadrants become reduced to exterior quadrants. This means we lavish attention on the exterior world and our interior world starves. This creates an imbalance inside us and in the way we perceive reality.

A recent survey revealed that most teens secretly desire fame and fortune. Their focus is almost exclusively on the exterior world. Likewise, the American Dream emphasizes chasing "bigger, better, more." This exterior focus requires a trade-off. We are invited to give up much of our lives and our convictions, often at the expense of other personal and professional opportunities, for the promise that we might receive a rare golden ticket to fortune and/or fame (which never turns out to be all we thought it would be).

In many cases, if we are honest with ourselves, we will see that when we were teens, we allowed the exterior world to seduce us. We traded our foundational, interior values for the empty promise of exterior rewards. As adults, we might have learned that we can ignore or discard our interior values for a while—sometimes even for a *long* while—but the compromise always catches up with us eventually.

I invite you to take a moment here to consider the amount of attention you give to your own interior life. As you move through your day, do you consider the values your thoughts and actions embody? How do your values factor in when you enter new relationships? When you take a new job or make other significant career and life choices, how deeply do you consider the values you hold in highest regard?

Many people have a place in their home or office where they can sit in silence to commune with the Divine and engage in daily spiritual practice. There, they might pray or ask for wisdom and guidance. We can call this place an "inner sanctuary." Do you have an inner sanctuary where you take your problems and opportunities, so you can sit with them before you make big decisions? People I know—including me—do this periodically throughout their day, as well as before going to sleep at night.

To me, a simple spiritual practice like this is critically important. If you wish to live a healthy and productive life, you'll need to "go within" on a regular basis. Oneness means we are on an *eternal* journey. It means life never ends, and it means information and guidance from a higher level are always available to us.

In Neale's *Conversations with God* book series, one of the most important messages is, "If you don't go within, you go without." Ken Wilber's work echoes this message. His elegantly simple model calls attention to these truths about human existence and other aspects of life. It truly is a theory of everything.

For several reasons, we decided to present Ken Wilber with the Spiritual Leadership Award in a private ceremony at Ken's home in Denver with only a small list of attendees. The members of the Humanity's Team Global Council who were with us for the ceremony were able to spend time speaking with Ken, who was a warm, gracious, and accommodating host throughout our visit. He answered every question at length and smiled for the dozens of photos he was asked to take with everyone there.

It was a wonderful event. Portions of the ceremony can still be viewed on the Humanity's Team website in the Spiritual Leadership Award section.

## 55
# DEVELOPING POWERFUL TRANSFORMATIONAL EDUCATION

During the summer of 2016, Humanity's Team entered a critical phase as a non-profit organization. Our journey had begun in 2003 with a mission to renew and restore humanity's connection with God and with one another.

Ours had been a movement born of the desire to fully manifest the beautiful vision God had shared with Neale Donald Walsch—as recorded in his *Conversations with God* books—of what the world could be, aligned as it was with the visions of other spiritual guides throughout history. Since we'd been so dedicated to maintaining the purity of that mission and message, we created free programming that mostly consisted of interviews with leading authors and speakers in the transformational education space.

Now, with thirteen years behind us, we had to admit that the world was changing rapidly, and we needed to change with it. People's preferences and values were in flux. An increasing number of people were less interested in free leadership interviews and more interested in online education programs that showed them how to better understand themselves and their reason for being here, as well as how to become spiritually fulfilled and reach their deeper potential as human beings.

At the same time, members of our full-time or near-full-time support team had reached the point where they would need to be financially compensated to be able to continue devoting their time to the mission.

Every member of our team was continually adjusting their priorities at home so they could invest their time in Humanity's Team. Now we needed to find a way to become more self-sustaining and supportive of them.

We decided to begin developing and offering powerful, authentic transformational education programs that would support the conscious journey. It felt like the right move if we were to have a chance of surviving and growing into our full potential. It also felt right that Humanity's Team should play a bigger role in supporting people on their individual journeys.

As I described in a previous chapter, we'd made a brief run at creating an educational program years earlier, but that effort had failed. I was a little nervous about trying again. On top of that, no one on our support team had the professional experience and technical abilities to build the necessary infrastructure and processes, nor the skills to market and deliver outstanding educational programs.

If we were going to make the necessary changes to grow into a leading online education provider, we needed to begin a massive effort right away. I felt certain we had to bring someone onto the team who had experience in such things.

To this end, I reached out to my older brother, Kevin, who had been a general manager for the Exelis corporation, overseeing a 150-million-dollar division with 300 employees. After a restructuring of the company, he was between jobs; I hoped he'd be willing to join Humanity's Team for a while to help us build the infrastructure and develop the processes we needed to reach our new goals.

Kevin had begun his career as an IT manager and had then moved into roles in factory process improvement and factory management before becoming a senior program manager and program director. From there, he assumed a business "profit and loss" leadership position. These roles all helped Kevin understand the unique aspects of each function and gave him deeper insight into how those functions snap together like a puzzle to create a high-performance organization.

Kevin agreed to step into this "God job" with us and help us to awaken the world.

# 56
# ACCELERATING CONSCIOUS EVOLUTION

In July of 2016, Kevin and I came together with the other members of our support team to strategize our move into online education. We needed to set our vision for growth, identify technologies we would need to deploy, and decide which processes we'd need to build internally. We also needed to determine what specific training the team would need, so they could fulfill their expanded duties.

Successful, for-profit companies were already offering classes and programs in the transformational education space. At this meeting, we set our intention to not copy any of their programs. Instead, we vowed to find novel approaches and develop instructional materials that were as fresh and leading-edge as possible. We wanted to provide highly focused content specifically designed to help people throughout the world accelerate their progress on the path of conscious evolution.

I had read research suggesting that one of the most effective ways to learn is through collaborative teaching, with two or three subject matter experts as teachers with experience in a central topic. Over the years, we had often gathered thought leaders in groups of two, three, and four to explore topics during our free events. Most programs in our industry are led by a single teacher; we decided that collaborative teaching was a direction we wanted to explore.

The biggest challenge in developing Masterclasses that involve two or three experts is that there must be synergy among the experts and what they will be teaching. It takes time to pair up synergistic partners, identify an important topic for them to explore in a unique way, and then develop a cohesive and effective arc across an eight-week program.

But when all the pieces come together, this kind of instruction creates a cascading effect where the students receive a transformation greater than the sum of its parts.

Our first education programs were focused on conscious business. As I mentioned before, with John Thomas' help, we had created the Conscious Business Change Agent (CBCA) training program. This program was designed to train professionals who signed the Conscious Business

Declaration and who were ready to roll up their sleeves and launch a conscious business—or go inside a conventional business and do the heavy lifting required to transform it into a conscious one.

Conscious businesses tend to have…

- Passionate, healthy, and happy employees and/or partners
- Satisfied and loyal customers and clients
- Prosperous communities where businesses are generators of jobs, supporters of good schools, and generators of well-being
- A virtuous process for stakeholders and supply chains
- Shareholders with strong returns both financially and in other kinds of "wealth"
- Cascading benefits leading to prosperity and flourishing for all

The CBCA program included a guest faculty of industry leaders such as Ken Wilber, Steve McIntosh, Michael Beckwith, and Lance Secretan. It attracted a good deal of interest when we launched it and produced graduates, but conscious business was still a new concept. That program proved to be a little bit ahead of its time. There just weren't enough people who were ready for it, so each time we ran the program, enrollment went down.

We then created more conscious business services including a CBCA certification program, consulting services for businesses, a community of practice, and more—but we soon realized we'd need to curtail these services until more people caught up with us and created a more fertile marketplace.

The reality is, if we are to survive as a species, all businesses will need to become conscious eventually. It's the only way to create a sustainable planet where humanity can flourish. There is obviously more work to be done.

## 57
# GROWING INTO *HOMO UNIVERSALIS*

By the spring of 2017, our cash flow at Humanity's Team had become very tight, so I began looking for ways to increase our revenue and stay within budget. Earlier challenges had miraculously brought forth something or someone to help us navigate through our problems and propel us to our next stage of growth.

It happened this time, as well.

We were working closely with Barbara Marx Hubbard on a number of programs, so we were delighted when she announced she planned to move to Loveland, Colorado to live at Sunrise Ranch, which was owned by the Emissaries of Divine Light network.

Shortly after she arrived, she shared with us that she was planning to create and market a new online education program. I offered to help her spread the word about it whenever it was ready.

It occurred to me that this might present a larger opportunity for both Barbara and Humanity's Team. We could mutually benefit from partnering on the development and marketing of her new program. I even envisioned that the program could become an extension of our annual Global Oneness Day Summit and Celebration. We felt we could offer Barbara a chance to further her program's reach and impact while creating a substantial new stream of revenue for both Barbara and for Humanity's Team.

It was untested ground, but I felt sure we could go much farther together than she could on her own.

Global Oneness Day is about helping people develop the awareness and skills to live a more conscious life. Barbara told us her new program would focus on conscious evolution and, specifically, the process of growing into what she called *"Homo Universalis"*—the next evolutionary leap beyond *"Homo Sapien."*

As *Homo Universalis*, we deeply understand that we are all one with the Divine, each other, and all of life, and we develop the habits and mindsets to live that way in every moment of our lives. To launch Barbara's program on the heels of our next Global Oneness Day was, as they say, a match made in heaven.

Barbara had been a student of three of the greatest spiritual and philosophical minds of the 20th century: Teilhard de Chardin, Sri Aurobindo, and Buckminster Fuller. She was intent on bringing together everything she had learned from them and from her own research and practice.

Teilhard taught that the direction of evolution is always toward greater consciousness, deeper freedom, and more complex and loving order. Barbara resonated so much with this idea that she began to refer to herself as an "evolutionary." Like her teachers, Barbara believed Oneness and unity consciousness were significant dimensions in this evolutionary unfolding. She even dubbed the current generation the "Oneness Generation," because we would come into these new experiences and develop the skills to carry our species further on our evolutionary path.

When I presented my ideas to Barbara, she was thrilled. She agreed to partner with us in developing her new program. We discussed all the possibilities and decided to frame her new course as a deeply interactive, yearlong mentorship program featuring special guests collaborating with her on specific topics. The goal of the program would be to train participants to become exemplars of how to evolve and develop; they could then train others while they served as role models.

Here's how Barbara explained it: "I have become aware that a new species is emerging among us. A new type of evolving human is appearing in every culture, discipline, and spiritual path. We are naming this new species '*Homo Universalis*,' and it combines our spiritual, social/vocational growth with our unprecedented high-tech abilities. *National Geographic* has named this emerging species *Homo Sapien 2.0*, and if we combine all our new powers, not only can we heal the Earth and free ourselves from deficiencies, but far more…we begin to envision a cosmic future of unprecedented dimensions in a universe of billions of galaxies. Our crisis literally is a 'birth' of a new species on this Earth and beyond. Given the existential crisis on Earth, and my own almost 88 years, I have been motivated to issue this 'Call to Awakening the New Species' now."

My brother Kevin was still our chief operating officer at this time, so he and I, along with Team Leader Dee Meyer, created a plan for an end-to-end educational program. We nailed down marketing, course delivery, and customer-support features.

Just after Global Oneness Day in November, 2017, we were ready to launch. We planned for the live program to run for about a year, and we reached out to leaders in science, spirituality, and community organizing and invited them to join us as special guests. More than 500 people enrolled in the program.

Unfortunately, the merchant services company that was to process our credit card transactions was not excited at all. We'd started our relationship with this company years before, when we received only occasional charitable donations by credit card. When the company realized we'd taken in so much revenue for a program that would be unfolding over a full year, they let us know they were concerned about refund requests. They suggested they withhold our revenue and only dole it out to us incrementally over the course of the year.

I informed them that the refund period was only two weeks from the day the program began, but they were unmoved. They insisted on sticking with their plan to trickle out the revenue we earned. We felt they were too big and powerful to try to fight on this matter, so we had to make the best of the situation.

Our agreement with Barbara required monthly payments based on revenues received, and we had our own payroll to meet. This unforeseen snag put us back into a cash-flow crunch. It didn't help that revenue from our conscious business programs was continuing to decline, and we were climbing a steep curve in developing the new professional skills we needed to succeed in the online education landscape.

Our marketing, pricing, and other processes were evolving but not yet fully formed. To say things were challenging is a sizable understatement.

# 58
# OVERCOMING ADVERSITY
# IN A BIG WAY

With Humanity's Team's cash flow in crisis, in early 2018, I flew to Salt Lake City, Utah, to join my good friend, Tom Dowd, for our annual meeting. We reviewed our charitable operations, compared notes, and served as sounding boards for each other.

Things were weighing on each of us. Tom had worked for decades to build an industrial materials company; now he was considering selling his ownership position so he could follow his heart and dedicate himself full-time to Christian charity work. I was struggling with whether Humanity's Team would be able to master the necessary skills to become a leader in the transformational education space.

After Tom and I spoke at length and gave each other deeply considered feedback, we both came away determined to make necessary but tough decisions. Tom would sell his equity in the company that carried his name; I would be completely honest with my Humanity's Team partners about my concerns.

When I returned home to the cold, hard reality of what we were facing, I gathered everyone together and we reviewed spreadsheets projecting revenues; they were nowhere near what we would need to even cover expenses. Our income was in a steady decline.

The new Masterclass we had launched in April hadn't been as successful as we'd hoped, a devastating blow that meant we had to create a plan to lay off everyone on the team, starting in August, unless things changed. We'd give them as much severance pay as we could afford, to help everyone transition to new jobs.

Our only chance of surviving rested on the new eight-week Masterclass we were preparing to launch in July of 2018. The program featured four leading scientists/researchers in the human-potential movement: *New York Times* bestselling authors Gregg Braden and Bruce H. Lipton, PhD, along with Deborah Rozman and Howard Martin from the HeartMath Institute.

The program was called "The Science of Self-Empowerment: Cellular Consciousness, Heart Intelligence, and the Untold Human Story." We'd developed the program over the previous year, with Gregg Braden taking a lead role. He had even brought the other three teachers into the fold.

Like me, Gregg had been part of Silicon Valley in the early days. While he was a geologist by education, he'd served as the first technical operations manager for Cisco Systems in the early 1990s. But just as I had, he'd chosen to walk away from corporate life, feeling compelled to do something with greater meaning and purpose. He told me he had never regretted the decision. Gregg has since gone on to become one of the most respected and sought-after experts and speakers in the world on ancient wisdom traditions and human evolution.

Gregg's own research had added important new perspectives about the evolution of our human species. He also discovered that present-day humans have unrecognized capacities, such as deep intuition and direct access to our subconscious, which can generate healing and self-evolution. His ideas were the foundation of the Masterclass.

Bruce H. Lipton is a biologist and former medical school instructor and Stanford researcher. He had found evidence that one-third of medical interventions create a "placebo effect." It is positive thinking that creates the healing placebos produce. Bruce is renowned as a pioneer in the emerging field of *Epigenetics*, which explains not just what genes we have but how they are expressed. Understanding differences in gene expression allows us to comprehend how traumas of our ancestors can affect us even today and how consciousness can have dramatic effects on the health of our bodies.

For their part of the Masterclass, HeartMath leaders Deborah Rozman and Howard Martin brought innovative technology that allows people to shift their heart rhythm, to improve emotional well-being and facilitate clearer thinking.

In addition to the "The Science of Self-Empowerment" Masterclass, we also had created three, sixty-minute online video events to preview the teachings from the Masterclass instructors. We invited the public to watch these, free of charge. The idea was to spend forty-five minutes reviewing the scientific research and ways this research could be deployed in our daily lives; then, in the final fifteen minutes, we'd offer a preview of the new Masterclass so those who were excited about what they'd just learned could go deeper by registering for the eight-week program.

Statistically, only one in ten of those who view such a free online program then registers for the tuition-based Masterclass program that follows it. But because Humanity's Team is a non-profit committed to supporting conscious living worldwide, we felt it was important to share valuable tools during these free programs. We wanted those who attended to come away feeling they'd received something of value in the time they'd spent with us.

Immediately after we aired these free video programs, we began receiving requests for transcripts of the events. We knew we had fulfilled that intention of giving our viewers something of value.

On top of those requests, hundreds of people registered after the first of the three free online events! Registrations continued to pour in for weeks until registration closed.

After the eight weeks of the Masterclass were complete, we received a tremendous number of notes and emails from participants telling us how much they loved the program. The launch was an enormous success. By the end of the summer, we were in a totally unexpected position: We had made enough money to compensate our team for another several months as well as pay off our Humanity's Team credit card bill, which was topping $50,000.

We were, of course, still only one failed campaign away from going out of business—but we had generated the money to keep most of our team. Inspired, we planned to create more Masterclasses following this same model. We all felt more hopeful when we looked to the future.

This all underscored yet again the reason we use the term "God job" to describe what we do at Humanity's Team. The business continually survived near-death experiences, allowing us to continue to focus on our larger mission. Each miracle helped us renew and restore our own connection with God and with each other. The odds had been against us, but somehow, we came out the other side victorious.

Coming this close to losing Humanity's Team was nerve-wracking for me, but once I got to the other side, I felt only gratitude that I'd been guided and relief that I had persevered.

As you move through your own life, I encourage you to watch for signs, both within you and outside of you. If you feel God or the universe is charging you with a mission to help other beings or the planet in some way, trust that you'll also find the resources to carry out that mission.

The path to your goal may be unpaved, with rough, rocky terrain. You might encounter mighty temptations to stray from it—but every "God job" creates its own miracles. Whenever I have put my trust in the Divine and made the commitment to reach my destination, I've been surprised to find that things fell into alignment and the way became clear.

Proverbs 29:18 in the Bible says that "when it's God's vision, it always comes with His provision." I have found this to be true throughout my life.

# 59
# LAUNCHING THE 'CONSCIOUS LEADERSHIP' MASTERCLASS

On the heels of this success, my brother Kevin let me know it was time for him to move on. He needed to look for a job in the private sector that was more in line with his background and experience. He had proven himself to be invaluable during his time with us and we were sad to see him go. Shortly after he left, he was recruited to become the program director for a government contractor.

We turned our attention to planning our next Global Oneness Summit and Celebration, which was coming up in October of 2018. Over the years, Global Oneness Day had grown into an enormous production. Our team put in hundreds of hours each year to plan and implement this powerful, day-long summit event. We had to secure speakers who travel globally, and those individuals are often booked out more than a year in advance.

We also had to select relevant themes, pre-record panels, and then host the broadcast.

Global Oneness Day had become a year-round project. But because of this herculean effort, we were expanding our reach and our impact each year. We inspired critical changes in hundreds of thousands of lives.

When people see more clearly their connection and their Oneness, they extend the borders of what it is to be "family." Then, as a group, we take responsibility for humankind and the Earth—because we understand we are inextricably linked. We step into service to the world around us, functioning from our higher self rather than our smaller self.

You might have heard the expression, "Many hands make light work." When we awaken and come into service together, we see this adage coming true. We reprioritize our lives and take compassionate action together.

It's important to remember, though, that while there are worthy causes everywhere, we need to do only what we can do. One community project we care deeply about is enough. If we have big responsibilities at home with a child, a partner, or an aging parent, helping them may be where our selfless giving needs us to be.

We are each called to our own station in life and our own path of service. I believe that when enough of us find and live our destinies, we will at last be able to create the flourishing world we've dreamed is possible.

Global Oneness Day is designed to inspire those who take part in it, but one day doesn't give them the support to create new habits and patterns for living consciously. To respond to this need, following each Global Oneness Day Summit, we launch an eight-week Masterclass to support key messages that were emphasized during the summit. This helps people embody and express more conscious life-skills.

For 2018's follow-up program, we developed a Masterclass with Barbara Marx Hubbard called "Deep Self-Evolution." This program was a condensed version of her yearlong "Awakening the New Species" intensive. This class focused on her process for evolving into the new human, *Homo Universalis*. This new species moves from being passive observers of the world around us to being active participants in the process of creation. It supports a deeper, more loving and mature relationship with the Divine, our higher self, and the world we co-create.

Shortly after the 2018 Summit, I felt inspired to begin developing a Masterclass of my own that would focus on conscious leadership. I threw myself into creating a program that would not only train those who were just beginning on the journey, but also those who were at both intermediate and advanced levels in terms of their own conscious behaviors. The intention of this class was to help its students fully embrace critical conscious leadership skills.

I included all I'd learned from tackling the enormous challenges I had to face during my life's journey, including the U-turn from living the American Dream. I described my shift from enjoying the benefits of living in a community of other technology leaders in San Francisco, to releasing all of it so I could make room for more healthy and conscious choices in my home and work environments.

All of this has culminated in my new life, where I am working in harmony with a deeply vision-aligned team to create programs that now have an impact around the globe. I felt it was important to anchor the Conscious Leadership program in my personal journey, because I sensed this story would provide participants with insights and tools they might use to make the same kinds of shifts in their own lives.

As this Masterclass was taking shape, I reached out to the thought leaders I worked with on a regular basis, inviting them to join me for individual sessions during the program. As guest faculty, they could share their own experiences of becoming more conscious in their work and in their lives.

I ended up with an incredible line-up of revolutionary conscious leaders who agreed to take part.

Neale Donald Walsch joined me to discuss core consciousness concepts, the creation process, and a process for evolving the soul.

Barbara Marx Hubbard's daughter and sister, Suzanne and Patricia, joined me to explore aspects of following your calling and collaborating with others during the conscious evolutionary journey.

Michael Bernard Beckwith shared his unique process for living in Presence, and Patricia Cota-Robles talked about the power of inspiring others to more fully embrace the act of Presence in their lives.

Gregg Braden, Lynne McTaggart, and Lance Secretan joined me to discuss their own development into conscious leaders, which included the critical processes of intention-setting and "heart coherence." They also shared surprising research into dissatisfaction in the workplace.

Dr. Jean Houston talked about her personal process for organizing her day to accomplish a wide spectrum of projects, including writing books, teaching, giving speeches, and developing new ways for people to accelerate their evolution.

Bruce H. Lipton, PhD, Lynne McTaggart, and Patricia Cota-Robles took on the task of exploring ways to transform our challenges into opportunities to evolve, as well as things we can do individually and collectively to create positive change, elevate the consciousness of the masses, and close the gap between where we are and the future we envision.

The active exploration of living in a conscious way—and especially the journey of conscious leadership—are both still young concepts. This means all of us who engage in these practices are "pioneers." We are like hikers in unexplored territory. I hoped the Conscious Leadership program might leave signposts that would make the journey easier and more accessible for those who would follow.

We launched Conscious Leadership in early February 2019. To introduce it, we again created a free online video event series with three, sixty-minute programs. The title was "Be The Inspiration, Be the Influence… Be The Leader." We invited those who felt inspired by the videos in the free series to register for my eight-week Masterclass.

The program is divided into eight leadership-development sections:

I. Hear and Answer the Call

II. Core Consciousness Concepts

III. Follow Your Calling

IV. Live in Presence

V. Lead with Intention, Heart Coherence, and Inspiration

VI. Make Each Day a Masterpiece

VII. Build a Conscious Team

VIII. Contribute to the Conscious Evolution Movement

This program launch was quite emotional for me. It felt like the culmination of my life's work up to that point, yet it was also something very new. I'd never been a professional author, speaker, or educator, so those roles took a little getting used to. I was sharing publicly my most personal challenges and successes.

Each week, the participants and I met live to review course materials and go over questions. Then we met in small, peer-to-peer groups to exchange ideas. I'd grown and learned so much over the past forty years, and I wanted to share everything of value I'd discovered about growing businesses from the ground up and launching them into the world.

Being a conscious leader requires that you genuinely care about others and go out of your way to support their growth. I asked participants to invest their energy in this aspect of leadership, even as they focused on their own growth processes. Dr. Claire Zammit, the cofounder of Evolving Wisdom, says, "We cannot become ourselves by ourselves." This is profoundly true. To grow into our full potential, we must come into community, where we will learn to both request and accept help from others, and to support them and other community members in every way we can. This is a practical way we can live consciously and encourage the same in those around us.

At the end of the seventh week of my Masterclass, I told the participants that I would not be able to be with them live for the eighth and final module. I had planned for a year and a half to take my fourteen-year-old daughter Sophie to visit Cape Town and the Kruger National Park in South Africa, and the final module would happen the same day our flight departed.

My two-week trip with Sophie was long overdue. I'd been volunteering for Humanity's Team for sixteen years, and in all that time, I'd never taken two consecutive weeks off. This trip was a much-needed mental rejuvenation break for me. It also gave Sophie and I a chance to bond more deeply before she moved further into her teen years and all the changes that come with the territory.

It hadn't occurred to me that I'd grow so close to the class participants over the first seven weeks of the Conscious Leadership program. Having to miss the final module was painful. I was sad I couldn't share that culmination of the program with them face-to-face on Zoom. I wanted to wish each of them the best on their separate journeys.

The participants were all very understanding, and I departed for Africa with their blessing, leaving them in the very capable hands of my Humanity's Team colleagues during that final week.

Sophie and I then enjoyed an adventure that we'll remember forever.

# 60
# A DEAR FRIEND TRANSITIONS

**B**ack home in Colorado, I got sad news. My dear friend Barbara Marx Hubbard had become quite ill following a knee injury, and her condition was quickly worsening.

She was eighty-nine years old and was in the middle of teaching the "Evolutionary Ambassador Academy" program we had developed together when this happened. She continued to meet with participants on Zoom from her Intensive Care Unit bed, her voice strong and confident despite her weakened physical condition. The day after one of these Zoom sessions, she slipped into unconsciousness and was placed on a ventilator.

The doctors told us that her recovery was unlikely. Her family invited me and other close friends to join them as they said their goodbyes and to be there when she transitioned. We sang and held hands in a circle, sharing prayers for Barbara's soul to manifest the highest choice. We were sure it would. The next day, her family asked doctors to remove the ventilator and she passed peacefully.

On April 20, 2019—the Saturday between Good Friday and Easter Sunday—her friends and colleagues at Sunrise Ranch in Loveland, Colorado, where she had been living for the previous couple of years, held a celebration of life for Barbara. They asked me to speak, and I was deeply honored to do so. During my speech, I discussed Barbara's ideas about our current planetary crisis.

Barbara often talked about how she'd experienced crises in her life, occasionally causing her to experience bouts of depression. At some point, she realized that whenever a crisis struck, it was a sign that something new wanted to be born in her life—one door needing to close before another door could open.

Once Barbara had figured out this dynamic, she learned that she could move quickly past any crises directly to the "something new" by simply not fearing and resisting the crisis, as she had always done in the past. She believed this same dynamic existed within the evolution of humanity. The last years of her life were a mission to spread this message and train others to use the method.

I closed my speech by encouraging everyone at the ceremony to continue Barbara's legacy by following her lead and doing everything we can to assist in this birth of a New Humanity, to create a flourishing world in this generation.

## 61

# HITTING ON ALL CYLINDERS

During the spring of 2019, Humanity's Team began to hit on all cylinders. Both the Conscious Leadership program and Barbara's Evolutionary Ambassador Academy program were successful. We received overwhelmingly positive feedback from participants. The groundwork we'd laid over the previous year or so had helped, and so had the addition of three key team members who greatly assisted us during our growth phase.

Throughout our programs, a consistent theme is that we are *all* leaders, without exception. Each of us has unique powers and skills to share, and becoming fully conscious is the first step toward being guided to the station in life that is truly fulfilling and uniquely ours. The second step is to become a conscious leader to others in your station, modeling exemplary behavior and sharing your skills for the benefit of all.

Our programs are focused, in at least some way, on training participants in this process. Some participants come to us as seasoned professionals looking only to augment their skills, while others are initially reluctant to identify as leaders because they've never really seen themselves that way. We know from the feedback we've received that these "new leaders" leave our programs with a clearer understanding of the way the universe works, an expanded awareness of their own possibilities, and enhanced skills that will help them deepen their conscious journey and accelerate their evolution.

Our team had started working on a new Masterclass in mid-2018 called "Healing the Past" with a world-renowned spiritual healer, Thomas Hübl, and Dr. Joan Borysenko, the author of the *New York Times* bestselling book, *Minding the Body, Mending the Mind*. We were ready to bring it to market in 2019. This program was unfamiliar territory for us, focusing on specifically healing various kinds of trauma at the individual, intergenerational, and collective levels.

This Masterclass continued the success we had experienced with our other recent programs, giving us the much-needed momentum to keep moving forward with our mission. When the class was over, we converted it to an on-demand format so people could go through the program at their own pace, anytime they wanted to.

# 62
# MOVING BEYOND
# MONEY-MAKING PURSUITS

One Sunday afternoon, I got sad news from my close friend Tom Dowd. He and his wife Josie had been visiting an important charitable organization in Nashville, Tennessee, when she had suffered a sudden and fatal brain hemorrhage. She was only 69 years old. This was a deeply tragic loss for Tom and his family.

Tom and Josie were scheduled to fly to Shanghai, China, a few months later for Global Natural History Day, where they would have judged a global youth leadership competition that had been started by billionaire philanthropist Ken Behring in 2011. They had planned to travel to Shanghai with Ken and his family on his personal jet.

Josie's passing meant they needed a replacement judge. Tom and the Behring family asked me to join them on the trip, and I agreed.

Ken Behring had grown up in Monroe, Wisconsin, in a Depression-era home and found his first success by selling cars before moving on to property development. He eventually became a billionaire by building housing in Florida and California. He also bought and sold the Seattle Seahawks NFL football team.

Ken is famous for saying that he'd never experienced real joy until he began giving away wheelchairs to people who were not mobile. He started an organization called the Wheelchair Foundation and then followed with other charitable enterprises. These quotes of Ken's reveal a man transformed by philanthropy:

> *"In the years since I founded the Wheelchair Foundation, I have participated in hundreds of wheelchair distributions and have had thousands of moving experiences. I've met remarkable individuals who somehow managed to endure in a world that offered them little hope or meaning. I have watched their lives suddenly become transformed by a simple gift that gave them independence and mobility."*

*"I've never been an emotional person, but the simple act of giving had allowed me to open my heart."*

*"Often the most tenacious and successful people will be those you least expect, those who play from the heart."*

Ken often shared a Native American proverb that he hoped might be his legacy: "We will be known forever by the tracks we leave." He also said his best years were between age seventy and ninety, when he had moved beyond money-making pursuits. His son, Jeff, shared with us that, especially in his later years, Ken had become a channel for God's grace, touching thousands of lives.

We were heading to Shanghai because Ken had created Global Natural History Day there to inspire the interest of elementary and middle school students in the natural sciences and history. In a yearlong program leading up to Global Natural History Day, students explored local, state, national, and world natural history around an annual theme, such as environmental protection. This included extracurricular projects that required extensive investigation, designed to improve their analytical and critical thinking skills.

In another strange twist of fate, the week before we were to depart for Shanghai to judge those final projects, Ken Behring passed away at age ninety-one. Due to his age and health, this wasn't entirely unexpected—but it was still a painful loss, and the timing was obviously unfortunate.

His family was clear that Ken's wish would be for us all to continue with the trip as planned. The competition we would attend was part of his legacy. One of his sons stepped in to take his place on our judging panel, and off we flew to Shanghai.

Four thousand kids had taken part in the competition. Each of them had carefully researched a project during the previous year and then had competed in local, regional, and national competitions to qualify for the international event.

The participants were as young as seven and as old as eighteen. I found their research projects to be thought-provoking and varied. I learned about the germination of seeds in different water configurations—including the acid-rain that is becoming more common these days. I saw research on plastic pollution, the physiology of a healthy body, support for rare bird populations, preservation of clean groundwater, our solar system, factors contributing to height during formative years, and much more.

Prior to arriving in Shanghai, I felt certain my role there would be as a teacher, but I learned so much from the kids and the other individuals and families I met and observed while traveling around this city of 26 million. I saw kids investing in themselves creatively, stretching and growing, and becoming empowered in the process.

At Humanity's Team, when we speak about "living in the unity of all of life," we are speaking about what I witnessed and experienced during the trip. From Ken Behring and his family to the young program participants and their parents, the trip was about nurturing and building relationships with an acknowledgement that we are all deeply connected.

## 63
# THE 10TH ANNIVERSARY OF GLOBAL ONENESS DAY

We wanted to plan something special for the tenth anniversary of Global Oneness Day. In the past, we had broadcast the panel discussions, one after another, for twelve hours on Global Oneness Day—but we knew very few people stayed with us for the whole event. This time, we decided to try spreading the panels out over multiple days, to give people a better chance to take them in. We began calling the event the Global Oneness Summit.

We kicked things off on Saturday, October 19, so we'd have a large audience with us right at the start. Then we broadcast three programs a day until the grand finale on Thursday, October 24, which was Global Oneness Day. Many of our country coordinators arranged celebratory programs in their countries.

Something special happens when thought leaders come together to talk about something very pure—in this case, that we and all of life are truly made in the likeness and image of God, the Divine, the universe, the cosmos, life, love, or whatever one is inspired to call it. This year was no exception. There were more than twenty informative and inspiring panels featuring more than fifty luminaries, including Michael Bernard Beckwith, Matthew Fox, Lynne McTaggart, Thomas Hübl, Jean Houston, Lynne Twist, Sage Lavine, and Christy Whitman.

We streamed the entire Global Oneness Summit free of charge over Zoom and on more than 100 Facebook pages that had signed up to receive it. Because of all these changes, viewer participation increased substantially. Our new, multi-day format was a tremendous success.

We planned to offer a masterclass immediately following the Global Oneness Summit, to support the process of living consciously and to encourage people to take a much deeper dive into the topic that we explored during the summit. The theme we'd chosen for the Tenth Anniversary Celebration was "Conscious Leadership for a Rapidly Changing World," which was followed by my Conscious Leadership Masterclass.

One of the most fascinating aspects of the Masterclass for me was the number of luminary members of my guest faculty—all seasoned and successful professionals—who shared about the doubts they had experienced during their own journeys to become conscious leaders and to realize their dreams. I'd grown up as a middle kid in a large family with limited financial means, and I had certainly experienced my own doubts on the path to where I am now.

We all struggle sometimes with insecurity about our potential. Yet I have learned that once we become deeply aligned with the Divine, there is nothing we *can't* do and no occasion to which we cannot rise.

## 64
# A GLOBAL STRUGGLE
# CHANGES EVERYTHING

As we were beginning to develop our next Masterclass in early 2020, the COVID-19 Coronavirus was introduced into the human population. Early reports suggested that the Wuhan area in China was going to see the brunt of it and the rest of the world would be spared—but soon, it was clear those reports were not correct. The whole world began to feel the effects.

Infections in the U.S. surfaced first in Washington, then in California, and then in New York. Infection rates and deaths began to soar so suddenly, people were in shock. As the weeks passed, we realized this virus might change the way we live on this planet. Almost every country in the world went into lockdown, limiting everyone's normal freedoms and behaviors. The governments encouraged people to remain home to slow the spread of the virus.

On one level, the virus has taken an enormous toll. As of this writing, more than two-and-a-half years into the pandemic, more than six million people have lost their lives to Covid-19. The lost lives, along with the psychological effects that isolation and lack of social interaction has had on children and adults alike, has damaged us in ways that will take time and care to heal. Vaccinations are readily available now around the globe, and while many areas are returning to a sense of normalcy, there are still dangers and concerns. The disease's effect on our lives is far from over.

Front-line workers supporting health care and other essential services have risked their lives each day since the pandemic began; some whole departments were wiped out, due to their proximity to infected patients. During the lockdowns, some small businesses were forced to close permanently. Whole industries were devastated, at least temporarily, as travel, dining out, and in-store shopping became too dangerous.

The devastating economic and psychological repercussions are still unfolding. Yet despite these losses, we also have reason to be hopeful. The forced sequestering and the economic pause gave us a gift of much-needed time for introspection and reflection. A friend of mine suggested that it is as though the universe had sent us to our room to consider the decisions we were making. The pandemic gave us an opportunity to reset ourselves, rather than pausing and then immediately rushing headlong toward harrowing times again.

The difficult circumstances that cause psychological trauma are often fertile ground for making necessary changes in our lives. It is possible for us to come through these difficulties with a new perspective based on a return to our deeply held values. We might find we have an increased desire for real health and well-being for ourselves and our fellow travelers—human, plant, and animal alike—on this extraordinary journey of discovery.

During this "pause," it became common for people to decide they no longer need "bigger" or "more" and are instead choosing "better." They want to do better in how they take care of themselves and others… better in how they slow down and spend quality time with their families, coworkers, and friends… better in how they steward the fragile planet that is our home … and better in how they grow closer to the God of their understanding, through themselves and the world around them. They are choosing to focus more on the quality of their lives in a search of greater meaning and a deeper sense of purpose.

The crisis has brought people back in touch with their core values. They are now deliberately reprioritizing their lives, thus accelerating their own conscious evolution. Conscious evolution is not about losing yourself to find yourself. It's simply about tuning in to the Oneness that is always present in the here and now.

When we make time to quiet our perception of the world around us, we contact the Divine within. We become more heart centered. We feel our soul's calling and we pay attention to it. We may find our true mission in life and move on from lesser priorities. This might mean leaving good-paying jobs that are focused on materiality to take jobs that offer more meaning and better life-balance.

Some, like McKenzie Scott— Amazon CEO Jeff Bezos' ex-wife— are contributing huge sums of money to forward-thinking, non-profit organizations now, when so many are in need. She and Melinda Gates announced a giving collaboration that promotes gender equality, higher education, caregiving, and support for minority communities.

To this same end, organizations are now reaching out to Humanity's Team, wanting to partner with us as part of our PACE (Planetary Awakening, Conscious Evolution) initiative.

Unfortunately, the media's focus on sensational headlines and disaster reporting pays little attention to this positive progress. But the truth is that more people are stepping out and stepping up. A sense of both shared interdependence and vulnerability is making it all possible. It gives us hope for the kind of momentous change we desperately need.

We have spent years laying a solid foundation for this change. So much of the hardest work has already been done. It's possible we are even on the back side of the hill, so to speak, and it might be easier going from here. We still have more to do, but we are moving in the right direction. I believe it is well within our reach at Humanity's Team to fulfill our mission to make conscious living pervasive worldwide by 2040.

Before the pandemic stopped us in our tracks, humanity had gone a long way down a self-destructive road. Our cultural obsession with financial gain created an enormous burden for our planet. Mankind has treated the Earth as a refrigerator stocked with consumable items instead of a cherished and sacred habitat and home.

Excessive carbon emissions are causing global warming, environmental degradation, water and soil erosion, and countless other issues. The good news is, we can change the way we live to keep us from certain peril as a species. Maybe we're being given a second chance to take a more sustainable, compassionate, and caring path in our walk upon the Earth.

The myth of the American Dream seduced us years ago with its unsustainable "bigger, better, and more" obsessions and its salaries based on marketplace demand and competition. Intrinsic value is often no longer even considered as a factor. Along with systemic classism and racism, the obsessive pursuit of material gain has led to extreme and unprecedented income inequality throughout the world.

While there are people still desperately pursuing their piece of that dream, a great number of others are looking to replace it with deeply held values and a deeper connection to the natural world and to the Divine. They want to move in flow with the core rhythm of life itself.

Covid-19 can be seen as a great teacher that has come to show us how interconnected and similar we are, with our shared vulnerabilities. And while the presence of this terrifying killer has stirred up long-buried fears that have been building for decades, its true message might be about the value of compassion, unity, and love. It is only through those gateways that we will overcome our current challenges and create a better world together.

Love will prevail over our fear. The more we show love to ourselves and those around us—even those in far-off lands whom we will never meet—the more that love will bring us together. Love can ripple out in every direction, eventually touching everyone.

Those who want to profit from division have preyed upon our fear, and this has driven us apart. Only love can keep us sane, heal those wounds, show us what is of real value in our lives, and finally bring us back together.

My partners all over the world and I have focused on raising awareness about all of this for the past nineteen years. This is the work of our Humanity's Team 501(c)(3) non-profit organization. It is unfortunate that we couldn't take a less painful path to reach this place. It has taken a pandemic, excessive consumerism, and the global warming crisis—together—to become the catalyst for our collective conscious journey.

We must now take advantage of this groundswell of momentum to do what is needed to create a sustainable and flourishing planet.

The success of Humanity's Team's next Masterclass program further cemented my belief that we are up to the challenge of this momentous time in our history.

## 65
# TECHNOLOGY, CONSCIOUSNESS, & EVOLUTION

O ur "The Science of Self-Empowerment" Masterclass had made a huge splash in the transformational marketspace in 2018. It was still a unique offering in many ways in 2022 (at the time of this writing). Participants told us the wealth of insights they experienced in the class had a deep impact.

The success of this class inspired me to reach out to Gregg Braden again, to see if he might be willing to brainstorm with me on other science-based themes. Gregg wanted to work on the idea that the increasing role of technology was likely to interrupt our natural evolution and prevent us from accessing our higher abilities.

It is trendy this year for young people to use the term "sick" to describe things that impress and excite them. Gregg told me that young people often approached him at his public appearances and asked about the "sick" new inventions that can be implanted directly into the brain to give us extended powers. While he understood their enthusiasm, he also saw the potential danger. He was trying to think of a way to counter the entrepreneurs who were evangelizing these new technologies.

We decided to develop a Masterclass to examine our evolving human potential from a scientific perspective. We would blend ancient wisdom and leading-edge contemporary research. We named the eight-week class "Technology, Consciousness, & Evolution: Discover How to Unleash Your Ultimate Potential." The free promotional video series preceding it was "Smarter, Stronger, Faster: Discover Why You Don't Need Technology to Take A Giant Leap Forward in Human Development."

While there were a couple of other programs in the transformation space that focused on tapping into our superhuman abilities, this new Masterclass approached the subject from a fresh perspective. Our class also had the distinction of being taught by Gregg and Bruce H. Lipton again, along with acclaimed researcher Lynne McTaggart, author of the *New York Times* bestselling book *The Power of Eight: Harnessing the Miraculous Energies of a Small Group to Heal Others, Your Life, and the World.*

Early in her career, Lynne had recovered from an illness using alternative medical approaches, and her subsequent investigative reporting and work as a researcher launched her deeper inquiry into the nature of humanity and reality. She became a spokesperson on consciousness, the new physics, and the practices of conventional and alternative medicine. This made her an ideal partner for Gregg and Bruce in the Masterclass.

At the time of this writing, "Technology, Consciousness, & Evolution" has grown into one of our most successful programs, as it has introduced a powerful and timely alternative to transhumanism.

## 66
# THE POWER OF LOVE

While we were developing the "Technology, Consciousness, & Evolution" class, we were also planning our 11th annual Global Oneness Summit on October 24, 2020. The world had changed because of the Coronavirus pandemic, but also because of the worldwide protests against racism and police brutality that were set off by the very public and horrific murder of a black man named George Floyd by police officers in Minnesota.

A fiercely polarized political battle for the U.S. presidency also raged throughout the summer, and wildfires devastated forested areas all over the country, leaving hundreds of millions of dollars in damage in their wake.

We wanted to offer as much healing energy into that toxic mix as we could. We chose the theme "The Power of Love: Resetting Humanity to a New Way of Living on the Earth" for the summit. Because of our focus on love, we chose the *New York Times* bestselling author and spiritual teacher Marianne Williamson to deliver our keynote address. Williamson had just come off her historic run for the Democratic nomination for president on a platform of love, which carried that message into mainstream America. We also presented her with our Humanity's Team Spiritual Leadership award shortly before the summit.

To draw attention to the weeklong summit and its message of love, we added a special event called International Shout Out Love Day. Our team member Brian Christopher Hamilton had been working on this idea for years, and the timing seemed perfect.

International Shout Out Love Day asked everyone who cared about the future of humanity and the planet Earth to step outside at the same time—we chose Saturday, October 17, 2020—and shout the word "LOVE" into the sky. We wanted it to become an annual event aimed at bringing the world together, to create a kind of *Horton Hears a Who* moment as a show of global unity and connection.

With the Covid lockdowns still in place, we covered the event online via Zoom and Facebook Live. To make it possible for more people around the world to join us, we planned for two "Shouts," one at Noon Eastern Time, and the second twelve hours later, at Midnight Eastern Time.

Both events were wonderful successes. Tens of thousands of people from all over the world shouted their love at the sky. We did it again in 2021; as of this writing, we're preparing for the Shouts of the 2022 Summit.

## 67
# THE UNIFIED FIELD AND ITS
# ASTOUNDING IMPLICATIONS

O ur next new program, "Forbidden Science," centered around breakthrough scientific discoveries that have changed the story of our place in the universe and how we came to be here. These discoveries have important implications for our past and our future. Like two of our earlier programs, this one also features the brilliant visionary scientist Gregg Braden, this time paired with his good friend, leading unified physicist Nassim Haramein.

I wrote about Gregg in an earlier chapter, but I've only mentioned Nassim in passing until now. For the past thirty years, he's been a leading researcher in his field; he's also doing important research in mathematics, cosmology, quantum mechanics, biology, and chemistry. His findings— which have been published in peer-reviewed scientific journals—focus on a fundamental geometry of space that connects everything, including all of us, from the quantum and molecular scale to cosmological objects in the universe.

His latest research explores the mechanics and evolution of the universe itself. Nassim contends that the field of physics has been stagnant and without innovation for decades; his work had begun to steer physics in a new direction. He also delves deeply into the evolution of protons, atoms, and cells—and how biology emerges when cells begin to self-organize and evolve into biological structures with a system of consciousness that becomes self-aware.

The equations he uses in his research also predict, with thirteen-digit accuracy, the fundamental constants of the universe used in physics today, unifying all scales and giving us a roadmap or "user's guide" to the universe.

The research and archeological discoveries Nassim and Gregg share in the "Forbidden Science" Masterclass—much of which the insular, traditional scientific community is suppressing and ignoring—along with some of the other scientific research I talked about earlier in the book, open the door to potentially astounding implications.

What if humankind—you, me, and everyone—were designed to be in service to each other and to the universe as a whole? What if animal life and plant life and the planet itself were also designed to be in service? What if we are physically, mentally, emotionally, and spiritually designed for this role?

The results of Nassim's research show that we are all part of a unified field and that this field exists within every part of the whole, no matter how small, right down to the protons inside our atoms. We can access this field through our own bodies and minds, which are extensions of the universe discovering itself through us.

A functioning body is composed of trillions of cells organized into organs essential for our survival. Each system in our bodies works together with all the other systems to keep us functioning and healthy. The body's basic design is that each part of the body is in service to the whole.

Could it be that the cosmos has precisely the same design?

Nassim's research shares that the cosmos is a *holon*, meaning we (and everything else in the universe) are simultaneously a whole, in and of ourselves, as well as a part of a larger whole—and the connection, wisdom, and power of that larger whole also live in every part.

I believe his research suggests that each part of the universe is designed to nurture and support subsystems and the entirety of the whole. Also, all material and non-material objects in the universe work together to serve both subsystems and the whole—which brings us back full circle to my conclusion that we are physically, mentally, emotionally, and spiritually designed to be in service to life around us.

Could this be why those who retire to a life of luxury find something missing? You might recall the story I told earlier about billionaire Ken Behring, who finally found happiness and fulfillment at age seventy when he launched the Wheelchair Foundation. Could this be the reason so many people feel they are not living meaningful and purposeful lives?

Is it possible that, in uncovering the science supporting the design of the universe, we've uncovered our own human operating instructions? If so, there might be people who don't like it or agree with it—but that can't change the universe's foundational design and identity.

If you are not sure you agree, simply put yourself into service to the life around you, see how that feels, and evaluate what happens to you and those you serve. I have observed so many indications that we were designed to live in service to the whole, and now science is explaining why this is so.

Newtonian science separated us into discrete parts, and we assumed that was our identity. But Nassim's unified field theory and other important scientific research have put us back together again, where we belong.

In the "Forbidden Science" Masterclass, Nassim and Gregg provide an advanced peek into this extraordinary future for humanity, along with training in how we can be on the leading edge of that coming wave. Since its launch in December of 2021, this program has been incredibly popular. In fact, it may well be the most important program we've created yet.

If you're interested in hearing more about these leading-edge ideas, I invite you to go to the *Humanitysteam.org* website and watch a free program that features Gregg and Nassim called "Secret Scientific Discoveries That Are Changing Everything." Just listening to them discuss the implications of those discoveries can profoundly expand your consciousness and widen your perspective.

# 68
# GETTING DEEPLY IN
# TOUCH WITH THE DIVINE

Almost every week, I send out an email that I call a "From the Heart" to Humanity's Team's lengthy list of friends. I want to share a recent one of those emails that captures how I feel after all the years I've spent focused on Humanity's Team's larger mission:

Subject: Getting deeply in touch with the Divine

Dear _____,

When I read the morning news, most of what I see are stories about people wanting to move past the pandemic. They'd like things to return to normal; they'd like things to be the way they were before. This is even true for many people who were unhappy with their lives before the pandemic, because after the past couple of years, they simply crave the comfort of the known—even if it is unfulfilling. But there are others who see a gift resting quietly in the misfortune and sadness that currently enfolds the Earth.

Certainly, those who feel there's a gift waiting somewhere in this crisis also hold great compassion for those who are suffering and for the souls who, on some level unknown to us, have agreed to leave the planet during this pandemic. But there is more going on than the universal opening of hearts to others. Much more. I regularly hear stories of people who are finding time to go deeply within, to commune with the Source of All that Is—what we here at Humanity's Team call the Divine.

213

What a blessing it is that something so positive can rest side-by-side with a moment that is so incredibly challenging for so many. I hope you can feel into this blessing of deeper relationship and communion with the Divine, and that the gifts of this time are becoming clear to you.

Importantly, the internal whispers I'm receiving are not about materiality or prosperity, though those types of gifts continue to bless me, my family, and my work. Instead, the messages are about how we may have an attitude of reverence. They are about truly seeing the Divine expression and incorporating whole new ways of embracing and nurturing life.

I first came across similar ideas in 2004 while reading the book *Tomorrow's God* by Neale Donald Walsch. On that first reading, the impact on me was profound. When I read those same words now, the volume is turned all the way up. In fact, it's as if the messages reverberate off walls, ricocheting here, there, and everywhere, almost as if to say, "There is a time for everything. Perhaps the time for these messages has arrived."

Because they are still affecting me so profoundly, I'd like to share some of these messages from *Tomorrow's God* with you now:

*Experience the Divine as both Creator and Created.*

*Tomorrow's God (maybe now we call this Today's God)...talks to everyone all the time.*

*Some say seeing is believing, but I tell you believing is seeing.*

*God is the source of all Love.*

*God is separate from nothing, but is the All in All, the Alpha and Omega, the Beginning and the End, the Sum Total of Everything that ever was.*

*You must decide you are separate from nothing and act that way. One day you will be there, and you will have crossed the dividing line.*

*The message that God is separate from nothing is a radical message. Perhaps it is the single most important message of the New Spirituality... It is the missing message.*

*The world will change overnight. The idea that you and all humans are One with God and all life is psychologically and spiritually revolutionary.*

*The day of atonement, that is at-ONE-ment, is near at hand.*

What these messages tell us is that God and life are two sides of one coin, but we often don't see it that way. It feels to me that this is where we might have lost our way in contemporary life. We may, for example, pray to a distant god who seems to exist in the sky far above the clouds—but that type of god has no connection to the Earth. Certainly, that type of devotion doesn't recognize that the Divine is embodied in the Earth, in each person, and in all of life.

Or we may pray for the Earth as something sacred but separate from the Divine. There is a sense that we must do a better job of stewarding this planet—a precious gift given to us—but there is no sense that the Divine dwells deeply within the Earth, or that the Earth herself has a soul.

What if instead of seeing them as two separate things, we see the face of the Divine in life and see life in the face of the Divine? What if we were to renew and restore our connection with the Divine and each other? What if we were to not only believe that the day of "at-ONE-ment is near at hand," but also deeply experience this true Oneness and connection to all?

I feel this sense of renewal and restoration sometimes during quiet meditation and prayer. I hear the Divine whispering messages of reverence and inspiration in my direction every single day, and I hope you do, too.

If humanity were to believe these messages, just imagine the implications. Do you think we'd continue the pursuit of materiality at all costs? Would we speed by our children and nature in a constant race against time throughout the day? If we believed, *truly* believed, that "God is separate from nothing" and "God is the source of all love," might we voluntarily push the reset button as we come out of this economic pause and together—as individuals and as a collective—move in a new direction?

Do you think we'd become more present? Do you think we'd take more time to feel into the beauty and blessings in our homes, in our interactions with coworkers, when we walk our dog, and when we look out at nature? I'd love to hear the things that are in your heart when you take the time to commune with the Source of All that Is, or as I say, the Divine. If you like the idea, please take a moment to share with us on our Facebook page.

From all of us on Humanity's Team, thank you for sharing your inspirations and your heart!

In service to conscious evolution,

Steve

Steve Farrell

Cofounder and Worldwide Executive Director

Humanity's Team

I received so many encouraging and supportive responses to the above email. The feedback underscores just how many people are also paying attention to what is happening in the world around them and being inspired to move in a more positive direction.

People are sharing less about their material pursuits and more about family pursuits, charitable pursuits, and concern for the Earth. They are noticing the extreme movements of nature—the flooding, the hurricanes, the tornadoes, the algae blooms in the ocean, and the wildfires and smoke engulfing areas of the United States during the summer months—and they are shouting from the rooftops that we must take a stand soon to support the Earth and ourselves.

There is an increasing sense that we really are all in this together, which has led to a growing awareness that we must become carbon neutral by 2050. Some governments and organizations are taking serious steps to move us in that direction. Billionaire entrepreneur Bill Gates has published a book describing how we can reach the goal of carbon neutrality in that timeline. This shows that even members of the global elite understand that we are at a crisis point where we must all work together.

That work has begun. The United Nations, the European Union, and individual countries are stressing the need for carbon neutrality by 2050.

I see people focusing on deeper values instead of shallow desires. I don't know of a single person who is focused on getting a new and bigger house or a new, gas-guzzling car. Their priorities have shifted toward living more sustainably, helping others, and stewarding the Earth by demanding healthier food-growing practices and renewable energy systems.

The hardest part of creating momentous change comes from breaking old habits and shifting our priorities; only when we do so can we move in a new direction. For so many of us, this shift is already well underway and gaining momentum.

I invite you to take time regularly to examine your own life. Ask yourself if you are living in any way that runs counter to your deeper beliefs about life and the universe. If you find that anything is out of alignment, you can take steps to reclaim your inner harmony.

# 69
# THE FIRST HALF OF A LIFE WELL-LIVED

I'm now a little more than forty years out from my flight to San Francisco from the East Coast when I was right out of college. From where I was then, I could never have imagined the journey that lay ahead of me to get to where I am now, with all its twists and turns. I gained critical professional skills in my first West Coast jobs, striving for and experiencing the American Dream. Then I followed my soul's calling to cofound Humanity's Team with Neale Donald Walsch. I've worked shoulder-to-shoulder with partners from across the globe to manifest a new kind of world based on connection, unity, and service to the whole of humankind and the Earth.

It has been a road off the beaten path, for sure—but I see growing awareness of and interest in the conscious journey. Humanity's Team's transformational education programs, podcasts, blogs, Facebook pages, our streaming subscription service, our spiritual social network, and our other programs such as the Global Oneness Summit are all, slowly but surely, increasing the reach and impact of this foundational message of Oneness and love.

As of this writing, we have connected with more than a half a million friends on our Worldwide Facebook page and millions more through our networking partnerships with conscious leaders all over the world.

This decades-long adventure has been a journey into deeper meaning and a profound sense of purpose for me. When I started out, I had great enthusiasm and passion, but I was unsure of myself. I eventually learned to trust my instincts and judgment. Each success gave me the confidence to put even more of myself into my work.

My success in chasing the American Dream and all its trappings, as I became part of the Silicon Valley "club," brought me prosperity. And while it was exhilarating to meet and interact with so many bright, passionate, and purposeful people in exotic and luxurious settings all over the world, the most valuable thing I gained during that time was knowledge and experience. That life gave me more confidence in my own abilities.

One day, as I was immersed in that rarified world yet still apart from it, I realized I'd placed too much focus on my professional life at the expense of my personal life. I had lost my sense of what truly mattered. I knew then that I'd never truly fit in with that elite "club" —because it wasn't where I was meant to be.

I realized that while the American Dream I'd been pursuing would lead to greater financial prosperity, I was clearly being called to work that was deeply spiritual. It felt like work that was far more important, not just to me, but for humanity.

A powerful calling was taking hold of my life, a soulful inner journey to new levels of meaning and purpose. I began to feel a sense of presence, wholeness, unity, and awakened consciousness, and I discovered a deeply spiritual and interconnected ecology.

My friends and colleagues in science and research were exploring the frontiers of consciousness and describing the very same thing, but in less spiritual terms. They described this as a "field" that threads through all things, affecting all matter in the universe. They would often discuss quantum mechanics. Particularly, they would describe how tiny particles can become "entangled," and since our entire universe is said to originate from a microscopic dot in space, all the matter we see may well be entangled with itself. Often, this research described a deep resonance with the principles of quantum physics, which explicitly show that life is an interrelated, interconnected, and interdependent part of a single reality they often describe as "the Cosmos" or "life."

At that time, I imagined what the world might look like if children grew up deeply understanding these truths—how different things like personal relationships, civic duty, and personal goals might be. Would we continue to obsess about personal wealth? Or would we instead open our eyes to the sacred and revere the Divine? Would we seek to serve life first, instead of just ourselves? Might life on our planet look more like a holarchy in the future, where we are both intricately connected and in service to each other?

Over several years, it became clear that my heart was inspiring me to give my all to this new worldview. I realized it would be impossible for me to keep one foot in the Silicon Valley mindset and the other in this new way of thinking about things.

I knew I could not serve two masters, so I released my role and participation in material pursuits and began to fully embrace a more conscious way of living. I left behind the life I had built in Silicon Valley and moved with Stephanie and our children to Boulder, Colorado.

Since that time, together with my new partners at Humanity's Team, we've invited millions of others around the globe to join us in embracing this way of approaching life and engaging with those around us. I believe, unequivocally, that the world is more conscious because of it.

The growth of Humanity's Team and the feedback we still receive daily from the larger community bears that out in ways that are both galvanizing and inspiring. I am more confident than ever that we can reach our goal of conscious living worldwide in my lifetime.

# PART 4

A Look Ahead

# 70
# CHANGING HUMANITY'S FUTURE

As I write this, Humanity's Team is in its 19th year. While we were late coming into the transformational education industry, now we are taking a leadership role, pioneering innovative ideas and setting trends.

Every month, we add new Masterclasses and transformational education programs to our library. Each program focuses in a unique way on an important topic that we feel is unavailable or underserved elsewhere in transformational education. We spend from six months to a year developing each new Masterclass program.

We have introduced innovations in the industry including collaborative teaching and live mentoring for otherwise digital programs, so participants can experience the incredible value of receiving guidance directly from the instructors. Feedback from participants suggests that this element exponentially adds value to the programs and helps to catalyze more profound levels of transformation.

Our programs answer the kinds of questions that are vital to our further evolution as individuals and as a species:

- How can we heal from childhood trauma?
- How do we choose between remaining distinctly human or merging with machines?
- How do we become fully self-empowered?
- How do we embrace a higher love in our relationships?
- How can we extend ourselves beyond our seeming limitations?
- How can we better embody Divine consciousness?
- How do we become better, more conscious leaders?

- How can we regain the sense of awe and wonder we experienced when we were young?
- How can we deepen our creativity and allow it to be part of our transformative journey?
- And most importantly: How can we speed up our evolution into the new species we are destined to become?

The irony is that we needn't stretch beyond ourselves to evolve into this new species. The Divine is— and has always been—*immanent*, meaning "within us." We can always find our own Divine nature when we look inside ourselves. When we take the time to reconnect with that Divine nature and prioritize it, we are actively evolving into the new species we are destined to become.

This potential has always been present within us, but we often completely overlook it; when we discover the Divinity we embody, we treat it as the treasure it surely is. From that moment forward, we can express the Divine that flows through us. We become its arms, legs, and lungs. We become its expression in the world and begin living as that new species, finding and following our soul's true calling. Then we are guided to our station in life where our unique gifts can be given to others—in our own homes, in our communities, and in the world.

As I look into the future of Humanity's Team, I'm excited about the world we're building together with the goal of creating healthy and supportive homes and communities across the globe. When we see the Earth and the whole of the universe as a living system, and see ourselves as part of that whole, it becomes obvious that everything we touch, see, and feel is both Divine and a part of us.

To support the spread of this awareness, Humanity's Team is determined to stay on the leading edge of human evolution. We have important plans for humanity that extend into the next two decades. We recently announced the launch of a groundbreaking new initiative in partnership with Neale Donald Walsch's Conversations with God Foundation. It's called "Changing Humanity's Future," and its mission is to follow the plan God suggests, in Neale's own *Conversations with God* books, for uplifting humanity and the planet by helping people everywhere shift to living more consciously, both collectively and as individuals.

It is urgent that we start now, if we are to create a sustainable and flourishing planet. Humanity's Team is dedicated to doing everything we can to support people on this journey, so we can make conscious living pervasive throughout the world by the year 2040.

As I've mentioned before, this perspective and the steps for us to course-correct are fully aligned with the discoveries of modern science and with the sacred texts that have been given to us throughout history:

### The Changing Humanity's Future Initiative Action Steps

1. Listen to the still, quiet voice that is God guiding you from within.
2. Open yourself fully to your conscious self, to that which is your true nature.
3. Follow the impulses of your soul in every moment, embody your uniquely personal calling, and model that behavior for others to see.
4. Encourage others to follow their own inner guidance, as well.
5. Share both your struggles and your process on the path to full awakening, openly and authentically, with those whose lives you touch.

6. Create a *Reason*. The challenges you have chosen hardly seem worth confronting unless you accord them greater meaning than just the simple triumph over them. This is because your path is not without purpose. It serves not only your own agenda but the superconscious will of the collective, advancing the evolution of the species even as individual progress is attained.

7. Express *Gratitude*. This is the most powerful tool you have, as gratitude can be a deliberate outpouring of positive and generative energy rather than just a reflexive response.

8. Choose your preferred state of being. Do this in advance of anything you know you are going to think, say, or do, because through pure intention, "beingness" can be transformed from a reaction to a creation.

9. Go with the *Soul*. You most often respond to whatever is happening in your life – whether it is an illness, a disappointment, a happy surprise, or whatever it might be – from the logic center in your mind, but it is possible for you to cultivate the ability to respond from the wisdom center in your soul.

10. Self-identify as being an awake human expression of God's wisdom and Love.

For humanity to get on track to achieve our goals, we will need to pick up the PACE (which for us stands for "Planetary Awakening, Conscious Evolution"), and generate powerful momentum to propel us forward. Many of the world's thought leaders share our belief that humanity is now facing a severe test. Dangerous environmental challenges affect human health and the Earth's ecosystems. We must act now if we are to continue to exist on a planet where we can thrive.

In response to this crisis, we've created the "Changing Humanity's Future" initiative with the goal of helping to shift careless human behaviors that contribute to our devolution, replacing them with conscious practices that elevate us individually and collectively.

To achieve our bold but critical goals, the initiative focuses on making original, high-quality, conscious content available to people in every community in every country in the world. We provide this content on an economical, true streaming platform that hosts hundreds of transformational education programs and live programs including viewing parties and mentoring sessions most days of the week.

We designed these programs to help you grow, develop new skills, express more heart, and lead a more prosperous and happy life. For anyone interested in committing to the conscious journey, the service provides a wealth of opportunities for personal transformation, which is the first step toward our collective awakening.

We want to create a sustainable Earth where humanity can flourish. For a long time now, the mainstream of humanity has been disconnected from the natural world. Acclaimed philosopher of science Ervin Laszlo has observed that we are no longer aligned with the rhythms and balances of nature; instead, we have created our own artificial rhythms and perilous balances that ignore and often conflict with those of nature. We believe we can override the natural rhythms simply because we have electricity and modern technologies that let us live our lives on any schedule we choose.

Along with this conceit, our collective obsession with the American Dream and its "bigger, better, more" mandate is sadly still going strong. This "American" Dream has now become the global dream; people of all nations have learned about it through the Internet and want a piece of it for themselves.

Our youth often dream not about living joyful, enriching, and fulfilling lives, but of becoming rich and famous. Modern parents often even groom and educate their children in every way they can to ensure they can attend the best schools and make the right connections to fast-track them to high-income jobs, greater power, and even fame in TV, movies, sports, or music—if the talent is there to make that possible, and often even when it isn't.

Humans everywhere are already suffering the consequences that arise from this approach to life. It cannot go on indefinitely. Our individual immune systems and the immune system of the planet are obviously under siege, and we don't need to look far to see the negative effects accumulating in individuals, marriages, families, communities, countries, and the world.

The tragic and devastating effects of the Covid-19 pandemic served to underscore these issues. The virus forced us to take a step back and evaluate our priorities, to decide whether our personal and collective identities need a reboot.

Humanity's Team has, over the years, risen to meet the challenges we've had to face. We've kept our own priorities in focus and have become stronger for it. But there's no doubt we'll face a host of new challenges as we continue our journey. We've impacted millions of lives, and our team, our outreach, and our finances are sound and growing—but if we hope to reach the "Changing Humanity's Future" goals we've set, the next step requires that we evolve beyond the worldview that we are separate beings in a world of finite resources. When we believe that there isn't enough to go around, it pits us against our brothers and sisters in a misguided "survival of the fittest" approach to life.

If you can feel your deeper, foundational connection to other people and to the Earth itself, then you might have experienced the calm clarity and sense of support that comes with that connection. When you live your daily life in tune with that connection, you are less afraid, less anxious, and less stressed. You are more free to truly be yourself and pursue your personal dreams in alignment with the Earth and the universe that created you.

You also might understand how taking actions that help others and the planet not only honors that connection but also uplifts and empowers you to continue to evolve into the full expression of your Divinity.

This is the foundation of what I've come to think of as the "Universal Dream."

# 71
# THE AMERICAN MIRAGE AND THE UNIVERSAL DREAM

The version of the American Dream I had pursued for years was always a mirage. The idea was that you'd labor furiously and sprint up the ladder until you had everything you wanted, and then you'd be happy. But once we hold our goal in our hands, we notice others who have even more. Then we want more, too—and no matter how much we manage to grab, it's never enough. As soon as we reach one level of treasure, a new level appears that is farther out. We can never quench our raging thirst for more, which keeps that promised happiness just beyond our fingertips. This life is unsustainable and exhausting. Many who have spent time scrambling for and then living the American Dream will confirm that this is true.

The "Universal Dream" leads to actual happiness and fulfillment in life. In this dream, we recognize our deep connection with everything and everyone who has ever lived and ever will live, as well as with the Earth and the entirety of the universe. Everything we do and say reflects our awareness of that connection and our embodiment of that Oneness.

When we live our lives in service to that Divine Oneness of all life, we find the satisfaction that has remained out of reach. We are completed and nourished by it. We find opportunities to grow and evolve into higher versions of ourselves, which then gives us the capacity to be of greater service to the whole.

For our commitment to this loving dynamic, we are rewarded with an abiding happiness as we flourish in every area of our lives.

While the American Dream pits us against each other as rivals for limited resources, the Universal Dream is a conscious journey where we live every moment aligned with the Divine energy of the universe. We can always see the Divine in each other and in ourselves, which inspires us to nurture and support each other and all of life on this incredible planet that is our home. Competition becomes worthless and meaningless when we live in Oneness. Instead of competing, we feel inspired to love, care, and cooperate with one another.

As the American Mirage continues to show that it will never deliver on its biggest promises, more people embrace the promises and rewards the Universal Dream delivers on every single day. I believe the American Dream's time is running out.

This is my personal dream and mission, as well as the mission of Humanity's Team: We want to put the Universal Dream within reach of everyone on Earth. Each of us has the power to choose where we focus our energy; if we choose to pursue conscious evolution, we can free ourselves and the planet from regression and even destruction. We'll also step into expansive lives of deeper meaning and purpose.

This universal shift to conscious living is indeed the antidote to so many toxic problems that threaten the whole of humanity. While those challenges might initially target the most vulnerable among us, there's no question that if we look a little further into our future, our entire species is at risk.

However, if each of us accepts our place in the circle of responsibility and leads by example, taking a stand for positive change everywhere, we can help support health and well-being for ourselves and future generations.

We can make it possible to birth a New Earth.

As I mentioned in an earlier chapter, the late Barbara Marx Hubbard called this the next step in our evolution into *"Homo Universalis." Homo sapiens* are anxious about getting more material things; *Homo Universalis* will leave behind that fearful and small-minded way of thinking in favor of something more expansive and powerful.

As we more fully become *Homo Universalis* in the years ahead, we will perceive ourselves and each other, along with the Earth and the animal kingdom, in a new way. We will insist that our institutions support this new way of living. Businesses that embrace this transformation into *Homo Universalis* will flourish; Those that resist will fall behind and diminish until they become obsolete and finally disappear.

If you recognize that you are still in pursuit of goals that resemble the American Dream, I invite you to look into whatever connection you currently feel to the Oneness that is the foundation of life and all things in the universe. Are you able to feel a deeper possibility for yourself and for our whole species in the ideas of the Universal Dream described above?

If you feel that resonance, I encourage you to act from that place in everything you do.

## 72
# PERSONAL AND COLLECTIVE TRANSFORMATION

How do we get to the transformation of humanity? We can take this next step in our evolution when enough of us devote our lives to transforming ourselves.

This positive change is already happening, despite the media ignoring what is truly the biggest story of our lifetime. People worldwide are seeing this bigger picture and feeling their deeper connection with others and all of life. Some are making the hard choices to move forward. They are letting that perspective guide their decisions about how to live on a day-to-day basis.

When you make a commitment to transform yourself, and to your own growth and evolution, you align yourself with the Divine energy of the universe. And through that growth process, you slowly come to understand that there is no separation between you and others and the Earth and the sky.

You turn inward and there discover the universe itself; that awareness then begins to inform the way you behave in your daily life. You become an instrument of compassion and peace. You focus time and attention on activities that have a positive impact on your life and the lives of others. You are mindful of the power of your thoughts because you understand that your *attention* is your *intention*. Rather than focusing on problems, you focus on possibilities, and you know that in giving, you also receive. And finally, you become a guide for others who feel inspired to transform themselves following your example.

Once you commit to living in this way, and you come into alignment with the Divine, nothing is ever the same again. You can never return to the limited way of living you knew before (at least, I don't know of anyone who has turned around and gone back to a lower level of consciousness). You understand that your life is not about you but about all those whose lives you touch. You concentrate on closing the gap between where you are in this moment and your vision for the future you're committed to creating, because you understand that the future is decided by the small choices you make every day.

The further along this more conscious path you tread, the more the universe seems to encourage your dreams and your actions, delivering new opportunities to help you continue your growth momentum. You begin to see more clearly and how to best use those opportunities, and while you do so, you feel more connected, blissful, and fulfilled.

You become inspired to jump out of your comfort zone in search of experiences that enrich you and others, feeling ever-deeper levels of compassion for all people and things. Your fear of physical death—the great dividing line that you cross at the end of your physical life—falls away. You focus less on what you're *doing* and more on who you are *being*.

You find yourself wanting to be in that "being" state where you are most aware of who you truly are, aligned with the Divine and prepared to do your best in whatever way it guides you. I believe this "being" state is what Jesus was referring to when he said, "The Kingdom of God is within you."

The true power of conscious living is that it creates a new kind of culture based on collaboration. Rather than championing individual achievements and promoting the idea of "everyone for themselves," this new culture promotes decision-making based on honoring our connection and choosing actions that are best for everyone and for the Earth itself. We no longer feel the need to create Newtonian, "survival of the fittest" alternate realities. We outgrow our desire for fame, fortune, and power. We move away from reflexively and exclusively "thinking things through" to make decisions, and instead intuitively "feeling into things."

We allow our intuition to steer us more often to doing what is most in alignment with our connection to each other and to the Earth. We also shift toward being more *relational* in our approach, knowing that a *transactional* approach all too often leads to blatant materialism and disregarding others' needs.

I hear more stories these days of people choosing connective goals rather than simply trying to build a bigger bank account. I hear stories of people fleeing lucrative jobs on Wall Street and finding work where there is more life balance and less stress. I hear people speak about their deeper priorities.

I hear about families identifying charitable projects where even teens can become involved, like the one my sixteen-year-old daughter supports, called "Golden Girls Global," which focuses on women's hygiene in Sub-Saharan Africa—or "Aid Still Required," the one my friend, bestselling author Debra Poneman, champions. They give support to areas of natural disaster and human crises after media coverage fades.

We might not see these stories highlighted in the press, but at Humanity's Team, we are surrounded by stories of people connecting with their deeper values, going within, and seeing the sacred. We hear of people choosing new priorities, moving to new jobs and moving from crowded cities to more peaceful locales. Despite the challenges we face as individuals and as a species right now, I feel a tremendous amount of hope in the air!

Our lifelong journey to becoming fully conscious *transforms* us; as our awareness expands, we understand we are so much greater than our physical existence on Earth. We sense and experience that we are limitless, spiritual beings, merely inhabiting our present human bodies for the exciting adventure offered by our time here. And we discover that the underlying feeling that comes from living in this new way—and that now drives our thoughts and actions—can be best described as *love*, the most powerful force in the universe.

When we fully embrace and live inside that feeling, allowing it to inform and inspire everything we do, abundance comes to us and others, and we experience a level of joy and peace we never knew was possible.

# 73
# ADDRESSING OUR WORLD'S CURRENT CHALLENGES

When we look around today's world, we see behavior that does not embody higher states of consciousness—but if we look harder, we will notice so many people who *do* live according to those higher states. Evolution is obviously a process.

The fact that so many people have chosen to take a more conscious approach to their lives means this transformation is possible for any member of our species. But the catalyst for one person's transformation may not inspire the same result in another person. Our unique gifts, talents, and skills, different life experiences, and the environments in which we were raised mean that humans are diverse. Each of us might need a different process to find the revelations and epiphanies that shift us to greater conscious awareness.

Evolution often involves healing from past psychological wounds. We also need to take current issues like nationalism, populism, polarity, hate, deceit, poverty, and exploitation into account. In the middle of all this negative energy, how can people who are living consciously encourage a global awakening?

Perhaps our most important role will be to model conscious behavior for those who are wanting to explore this journey. This means living intentionally and always doing our best. This does *not* mean that we hold ourselves up as examples of evolutionary excellence, because we are not this. We may have made great strides, but most of us would say we have a considerable number of things to work on. This also means choosing, making important life decisions, but not condemning other choices. Who are we do sit in judgement of others and the choices they make?

We try to be alchemists, healers, and guides. We try to speak our truth, show compassion, and help anyone in need, in any way we can. Those of us who share these goals for humanity are sometimes called "utopian" or accused of "wearing rose-colored glasses." People might assume we are foolish about the enormity of the challenges we face. We are trying to accelerate evolution in those who don't even realize this kind of change is possible or who cannot comprehend that there is another way to live, beyond the limited ways they've learned about and seen in others.

People have told me that I'm being naive to strive for reaching this goal in my lifetime—but I agree with Abraham Lincoln's idea that once we've determined that something is possible, all that is left is to find a way to make it so.

Even when a goal seems completely beyond us, if it is the right goal, all we can do is try to figure out how to achieve it. Humanity's Team was founded on this principle. We believe that only awakening to our interconnected world and our deeper selves can fulfill us and allow our species to evolve to the next stage. We've been working tirelessly toward that goal for years, and we are making progress and creating momentum.

Eventually, a breakthrough will open the floodgates for conscious living worldwide. The very nature of expanded awareness involves continuing to raise our own consciousness and helping to raise the consciousness of others.

For fifty-seven consecutive nights in 1940, during World War II, Nazi Germany aircraft released bombs over the city of London, hoping to break the spirit of the British people and their allies. But every day, Prime Minister Winston Churchill would visit the areas that had been blown up the night before, and he'd encourage photographers to take pictures of him smiling and flashing the "V for victory" sign. These photographs both inspired the British people and their allies and they showed Hitler that the psychological victory he was hoping for would never come.

Churchill's unwavering confidence and good spirits in the face of those nightly horrors deserves much credit for the Allied Forces eventually prevailing against Germany and its partners in crime. This is just one instance where leading by example helped people overcome tremendous odds.

We can see signs all around us, right now, that more people are waking up. At Humanity's Team, we feel we are gaining momentum. At a recent World Economic Forum in Davos, Switzerland, Marc Benioff—the billionaire founder of Salesforce.com—said, "Capitalism as we know it is dead." He also said that business leaders now have a responsibility to think beyond their shareholders, and that the "obsession we have with maximizing profits for shareholders alone has led to incredible inequality and a planetary emergency."

Benioff said that, as a CEO, he needed to fight not only for his company's employees and customers, but also for the community surrounding his company, including the homeless and others without resources. He had to protect the ground beneath their feet: "Every CEO has a responsibility to think about all stakeholders. And yes, the planet is a stakeholder."

Benioff is not alone in this surprising and hopeful perspective. His comments echo those of Dan Schulman of PayPal, who at the same forum said that business leaders had an "ethical and moral" duty to look after their staff. And the U.S. Business Roundtable, which includes top CEOs, announced that it was abandoning the idea of "shareholder primacy" and instead redefining the purpose of a corporation as "improving society." These are the kinds of shifts that will begin to happen more often as more individuals wake up to the truth of our deeper connection and the benefits of living a conscious life, not just for ourselves but for everyone.

You might not be the CEO of a big company, but the decisions you make for yourself and your family impact others and the world in important ways. The way you live might serve as a model for those who see you or hear you when you openly share your truth. The money you spend can send a message to those who supply those products and services that you are making choices supporting sustainability and inclusiveness. You can choose not to support companies that do not share your values and that are harming humanity and the Earth in the name of increasing profits.

Spending time in service to others or the Earth is one of the most powerful ways you can be effective. Nothing can send a more positive message about this approach to life.

# 74
# LIVING IN SERVICE

When we live consciously, we know and feel everything outside of our physical bodies to be a part of us, so our everyday actions center around being in service to those around us, including animals and the Earth. Doing things that help others or the Earth brings us joy, regardless of the time and effort we invest in doing this. We never think of it as a sacrifice because we care about others and the Earth, just as we care about ourselves. When this kind of thinking becomes ingrained in our nature, we feel grateful and deeply fulfilled by each opportunity to share our unconditional love.

Since Humanity's Team's founding in 2003, everyone on our support team has been in service to humanity. At first, we were volunteers. Slowly, we moved toward receiving market-based salaries, but always with service as the goal—never profit. We've lived in service to spiritual literacy, supporting people on their personal, conscious journeys, as well as our collective journey toward planetary awakening. We want everyone on Earth to flourish.

Individually, we've also been involved in other forms of service work, supporting organizations and campaigns that help the elderly and the homeless. We have supported animal rescue organizations and ecological and climate-change projects as well as programs like Meals on Wheels, There with Care, and Miracle Messages.

If each person or family in the world found just one service project in their community, and committed to volunteering even a small amount of time each week or even each month to that project, what might our world look like? The saying "Many hands make light work" is true. Feeling and following this impulse to civic duty is a critical part of the path that leads us to the creation of a New Earth and a New Humanity.

If you're not already living in service in this way, the first step is to identify what kinds of things are most important to you. It could be that you believe everyone should have access to unpolluted natural areas, or that everyone should have access to healthy food choices, or that people who are aging shouldn't have to try to do everything for themselves, or that endangered animals (or all animals) need human intervention, or that the oceans need our protection from polluting plastics.

Which of these things are important to you? Regardless of where you live, chances are, others or even entire organizations close by are already working on those causes. Service organizations rely on volunteers to support their critical projects.

It's important to repeat that living in service doesn't mean you have to give up your personal life and spend all your time volunteering for causes; it simply means that you spend time in service to others or the Earth each month, or each week, or even each day, if you have time to do so.

Service includes things like caring for young children or elderly parents. It includes helping others in any way without expecting something in return from the person you are helping. Any time spent in service is worthwhile. It always makes a difference. Be as generous with your time as you can be, and allow yourself to give less when you feel overwhelmed with personal concerns and commitments. Almost everyone can give something. No gift given in service is too small.

Every day, more stories pop up of people joyfully embracing this kind of responsibility and opportunity. It's like a pot of water beginning to boil. Just before the pot comes to a boil, bubbles start to appear and rise to the surface, letting you know that it will soon be boiling fully.

When it comes to conscious awakening, we are seeing bubbles! More people are obviously feeling connected to a larger tapestry of others throughout the world and accepting the mission to live consciously, connecting their life's work with the grand vision of a better future for all!

# 75
# CHOOSING YOUR PATH
# ANEW EACH DAY

As part of the conscious path, it's also important for each of us to look inward and figure out what we most treasure about our own lives. You need to define prosperity for yourself. Is there prosperity in your relationships? In your professional work? Is it in close, loving relationships with your partner, your kids, your friends, and/or your coworkers? Is it in your relationship with God or the natural world? Or is your prosperity in your bank account, primarily tied to your income, your investments, and your personal financial wealth?

It's important to decide this because whatever your prosperity is anchored to, that is where you place your attention and thus your intention. If your treasure turns out to be primarily financial, there is a strong chance that you will never truly feel prosperous. You will notice how much more others have or fantasize about how much more you could have if only you worked more diligently, had a higher IQ, or had insider knowledge about the tactics to get more.

The good news is that it is never too late to change. This is what I tried to do in my own life, and if there is one message I want to underscore here, it is that no matter how far down a path you've gone, you can always change directions. You can turn your life around and head toward happiness and fulfillment.

In truth, I've done this in my own life. I have found myself off course by a little or a lot. Whenever I discover this, I'm tempted to be frustrated and upset with myself, but I know there is no value in beating myself up over it. Instead, I've adjusted my course to the more true direction for me.

Once I've gotten myself back on track, I often realize the process has made me grow.

So many paths can deepen your connections to others, to the Earth and the universe that is our home, and to the Divine that is the source of everything. Those paths are never too far from whatever path you're on. They are yours to choose for the first time or to choose anew every day that you live.

You are here on the Earth on a mission of sorts. When you follow your soul's calling, it will guide you to your station in life. You will know who you truly are and how to best express yourself. Being fully devoted to your calling and your conscious journey requires the discipline to work on your mission every day to the best of your ability.

You are not simply a body experiencing a single lifetime and returning to dust at the end of that life; you are an eternal being evolving over lifetimes, an offspring of the Divine, with unlimited potential. Each day you will need to answer the same questions: How will I live? How will I feel at the end of the day about the choices I've made?

As an offspring of the Divine, we are the arms, legs, and lungs of the Divine, here to do the work only humans can do. Your job is to do the work that you alone can bring to bear in the world, fulfilling your unique destiny in each lifetime and over all the lifetimes you spend here. You were made this way, to be a healthy cell in the body of life around you. You will naturally feel joyful and excited when you fulfill the role you were born for; You will feel unfulfilled and out of sync when you instead make choices that are selfish and self-serving.

Matthew 6:33 in the New Testament says: "Seek ye first the kingdom of God and all things shall be added unto you." The *kingdom* is our sacred relationship with the Divine/Life. We can find this kingdom when we go in prayer, meditation, and stillness.

When we align with the Divine, everything falls into place. We find a new prosperity in more loving relationships with family, friends, and coworkers. We feel empowered to work tirelessly for causes we care about. We have a sense of being right where we're supposed to be, which leads to a deep, abiding peace. We can share this peace when we join hands and hearts with others.

When we make this manifest in our reality, we create a new humanity and a new Earth.

For the sake of transparency, and for perspective, before leaving Silicon Valley, I thought I had a sense of purpose. I enjoyed various rewards. Yet I never truly felt settled, satisfied, or at peace. Since shifting gears with my family and coming to Colorado, I've felt far more purposeful and more in flow. I know I'm doing what I truly came into this life to do, which is fulfilling my personal mission and doing my part for the whole.

As a result, my sense of cognitive dissonance is gone. The incessant tapping on my shoulder has vanished, along with the sensation of always craving more. The hole in my soul has been filled. I now feel a sense of prosperity and satisfaction far beyond anything I felt during my entrepreneur days in the technology industry. I believe this is one of the most important signposts on the conscious journey. At the end of the day, we feel full and alive instead of half-empty and depleted.

I am on my own personal journey. I have not reached some grand destination where I've achieved mastery of life, but I'm deliberately trying to evolve into the highest expression of who I am. I often push myself harder than I should, but it's because I'm passionate and devoted to so many things. To counter this, I'm paying closer attention to myself every day, reminding myself to take more breaks and laugh more with my team. I'm making more time to take longer walks with my dog and to just sit and enjoy the outdoors with Stephanie and our now-grown children.

My passion and enthusiasm even sometimes interrupt my sleep, because I'm so excited about the coming day. I've made adjustments to ensure I get enough sleep to be at my best.

These are just a sampling of the things I'm pursuing in my own journey. I believe this is the kind of work we all must do on ourselves as we seek to honor the gifts and opportunities we've been given by the source of everything there is.

## 76
# GIVING BACK TO THE DIVINE

As far back as I can remember, prayer has been a part of my daily life. Prior to my conscious awakening, I always prayed to a God I knew to be "up there somewhere," expressing gratitude for his gifts and guidance and asking for his grace for me and those I love.

After my personal awakening, my experience of God changed profoundly. I came to fully realize that God's Divinity was not only everywhere and in everything—it was also ever-present in *me*. I noticed how aligned I felt with that Divine energy when I allowed its presence into my thoughts and actions. This applied especially to anything I pursued creatively, including my personal journaling. I also began to experience that Divine energy more often in my outer world—in nature, in animals, and in my observations of other people.

I no longer pray to a transcendent God who is independent of the material universe, somewhere above the clouds. Now I pray to an immanent God who is always right here, right now, both within me and without. I view myself as a vessel for that Divine energy to express itself in the world.

I consider myself as a co-creator with the Divine, and others all over the world, as we try to raise the whole of humanity to awakened awareness.

Through this shift in my own practice, I've seen that small steps taken daily can lead to great distances covered over months and years. Many spiritual leaders I've been inspired by, including Gandhi, have advocated for this slow and steady approach.

Gandhi believed in the compassion illustrated by the Sermon on the Mount, when Jesus spoke of the need for solidarity with the poor and oppressed. Gandhi also believed all the major religions contained truth, but he felt they should adopt compassionate universal principles that transcend religion and dogma. In Gandhi's view, we cannot speak of oppression and injustice while we continue to support the status quo through the personal choices we make every day.

Rather than quick and drastic change, which is difficult, Gandhi advocated for slow and steady changes that make progress toward goals for the common good. One of his slogans was: "One step is enough for me." He believed that every step in the direction of the desired horizon would eventually lead us there, no matter how distant it might seem.

While few of us have Gandhi's resolve and determination, I've tried my best to embody that same belief in all I've done on my own conscious journey as well as through everything Humanity's Team has done. If we, as a species, can commit to those kinds of small, steady steps toward a world that works for everyone, we might be astonished at the distance we can cover.

We need to do less talking and start walking toward that better world.

This is how we can give back to the Divine, which has bestowed this opportunity and responsibility upon each of us: We can use the life we've been given to create something of value to the whole. We can explore our own highest possibilities in connective harmony with all that surrounds us. I encourage you to look for all the ways you can do this in your own life.

Take time each day to consider your own deeply held values and ways you can incorporate these into your decisions and actions in a steadily increasing way. It just might surprise you when you turn around—ten, fifteen, and twenty years from now—and see the distance you've covered.

## 77
# A NEW UNIVERSAL DREAM

The American Dream can seem to pursue us relentlessly. It is portrayed everywhere, in movies, television shows, commercials, and magazines, and even on social media.

Regardless of where we live in the world, most of us have felt that pull to pursue this kind of prosperity. It can make us hunger for greater wealth and luxury, a bigger house, a better car, the latest smart phone, a boat, a swimming pool, or fame or prestige.

The trappings of wealth aren't inherently evil. Being famous or admired by others is a common fantasy. But the relentless pursuit of the American Dream is an unhealthy trap, because no amount of wealth or success can ever be enough. We can find ourselves pitted against others who are pursuing the same dream while holding the belief that there isn't enough to go around—so someone else must lose for us to win.

The crises of our modern world—global warming, viruses, endless wars, and political upheaval—have shaken some people out of our pursuit of that kind of dream. We have begun to focus on more important things. The truth is that we are all part of the same Divine whole—not in competition with each other, but in collaboration. The only way for us to win anything is if the whole of humanity is lifted and elevated.

We must be compassionate and caring toward others. We must do whatever we can to help create a better world that works for all of us. In short, we must evolve together.

The good news is that many of us are fully embracing this reality and recognizing the positive possibilities, despite the many crises. Realizing this foundational truth is where the conscious journey begins.

While each of our journeys will unfold in a unique way, all of them will involve renewing and restoring our connection with the Divine, life, and each other. Recognizing our connection provides us with clearer intention and deeper meaning; living in recognition of this connection brings great blessings and prosperity, both financially and in every other aspect of life. Each journey will find us becoming more in harmony with life—but the forms this can take are unlimited.

We might still consider ourselves Christians, Buddhists, Muslims, Hindus, Jews, or something else, but we are likely to embrace those compassionate, universal principles Gandhi believed in. We will transcend religious dogma, race, color, and gender orientation to create an environment that is equally nurturing for everyone, free from prejudice or bias. We will give our common goals priority over our individual ones.

Unfortunately, sometimes our best intentions are stymied by a lack of direction. Even when we are heart-centered and feel called to service, we often simply don't know how to best spend our time and effort to be effective.

I've taken the following simple steps to support my conscious journey and help bring about planetary awakening and flourishing for all. I hope these suggestions might be of value to you as you search for your own path to fulfilling service:

1.  Go within daily—in prayer, in meditation, in nature, or using stillness practices—and nurture your relationship with the Divine or All That Is, using whatever name helps you best connect to that energy.

2.  Commit to serving life (including the natural world around us) first and embrace the reality that your life is about contributing to the greater good.

3.  Use the power of your dollar to buy conscious products that support sustainability and flourishing.

4.  Bring your personal and professional relationships into alignment with your soul's unique calling.

5.  Enjoy the many forms of prosperity that come back to you through this novel approach to your life and remember that love's expression is the grandest and highest gift.

We are here on the Earth to prosper and create fulfilling lives for ourselves, as well as a way forward for our children and their children, for generations to come. I wish the best for you on your conscious journey. If I or Humanity's Team can ever be of service to you, please reach out to us anytime.

# POSTSCRIPT:
## ABOUT HUMANITY'S TEAM

Humanity's Team was founded in June, 2003 in Wilsonville, Oregon, and is a 501(c)(3) non-profit focused on sharing the following essential truths:

- We are all One with God/the Universe, each other, and all of life.
- God is not judging or condemning but is instead pure love, in service to and empowering all of life.
- The properties of God/the Universe are our properties, including eternal life.
- The Universe is non-dual and in unity and harmony.

Education is key to social change, so Humanity's Team has created a revolutionary conscious streaming community and platform to share many forms of education supporting our conscious journey. These programs are part of our mission to make conscious living pervasive worldwide by 2040.

Since its conception, Humanity's Team has become the #1 global non-profit in the transformational education space, offering fresh evolutionary content, collaborative teaching, and live mentoring that is generally not available—at least at this time—anywhere else in the industry.

If you'd like to learn more about Humanity's Team and the work we do, I invite you to check out our global website. We've created year-round programs to support those who are on the conscious journey. Our website offers free, hourlong online programs, podcasts, blogs, and other transformational resources. You can also friend us on Humanity's Team, our conscious social network, and on our Worldwide Facebook page, as well as on Instagram, Tik Tok, Twitter, YouTube, Linked-In, and Pinterest.

Together with respected conscious leaders from around the world, we've created free, content-rich, online video and audio seminars, along with other programs. If you're interested in taking a deeper dive into their teachings, these programs also include previews of our affordable, tuition-based Masterclasses featuring those same leaders.

In addition, we've created a groundbreaking subscription platform called "Humanity Stream+" with an intuitive, graphical interface that includes access to our most popular Masterclasses and hundreds of other programs. This platform not only provides you with a supportive conscious community, it also puts you fully in control of your own conscious journey. You can watch the content from the comfort of any room in your home or when you travel, as it is available on IOS, Android, Android TV, Fire TV, Roku, and Apple TV. We add new programs every week.

Humanity Stream+ members are also invited to attend the live, online mentoring programs we offer regularly with new faculty, as well as other community teachings and practices. Following our annual Global Oneness Summit, you'll have access to replays of all the video programs for free, and you can also engage with the private Masterclass communities for each of the Masterclasses, join weekly watch-party gatherings with others, and receive free certificates for each Masterclass you complete. This subscription service is affordably priced, offers a monthly payment option, and is, at the time of this writing, the lowest-cost service of its kind in the transformational education industry. We also offer a fourteen-day satisfaction guarantee to give you time to explore all the wonderful benefits of our subscription service at no risk before you commit to an annual membership.

Humanity Stream+ is our strategic platform for inviting each person and the whole of humanity into the conscious journey and onto the path that will lead us to full planetary awakening. Because we are a non-profit, we have no shareholders, sales targets, or profitability measurements. Our whole reason for being is to support people on their personal conscious journeys, so that together we can create a sustainable, flourishing planet for the benefit of all within this generation and for all the generations to come.

We invite you to join us in our "Changing Humanity's Future" initiative—our plan to replace careless behaviors that are contributing to our regression with conscious practices that elevate us, both individually and collectively. Again, our mission is to make conscious living pervasive worldwide by 2040.

If you haven't yet found your "conscious" global tribe, we are here waiting for you with open arms. Half our members are in the United States and half live in other countries, but all of them are serious about living consciously. In our Humanity Stream+ community, we are open-hearted, we live in flow, and we hold space for each other to grow and evolve in our own unique ways.

We gather several times each week, and when we're not gathered face-to face, we're connecting with each other in our virtual community. This community provides us the chance to make new and diverse contacts with others, expanding our larger team as we work together to realize our highest potential as humans. I hope to see you there!

*www.humanitysteam.org*

# ACKNOWLEDGMENTS

As this book recounts my 50+ year journey from age 11 to the present, you can likely imagine, there are far too many people who contributed to my story to thank and acknowledge here, but I will do my best to thank as many of them as I can.

For assistance in preparing and editing this text, I'd like to thank Brian Christopher Hamilton, Neale Donald Walsch, Ross Hostetter, Tom Dowd, and Karen Gordon. I would also like to thank my agent, Bill Gladstone, my friends at Sacred Stories Publishing, including the publisher Ariel Patricia, and Kurt Johnson and Bob Atkinson at Light on Light Press.

I'd like to acknowledge my wife Stephanie, my son Dylan, and my daughter Sophie for being patient with me for all these years, supporting my commitment to embracing a more conscious lifestyle, launching and developing Humanity's Team, and through the time I devoted to writing this book.

I'd also like to thank all of my dear friends and colleagues at Humanity's Team, without whom my journey would not have been or continue to be possible. Everything we have created together has been a true team effort, with contributions from partners all over the world. In particular, I'd like to thank Dee Meyer, our Humanity's Team worldwide operations director, who has played such an integral role in nurturing the organization into what it has become today.

I'd also like to thank my mother, Linda Farrell Small, my late father Joe Farrell, and my siblings, who have been part of much of this journey with me, Monica Rawles, Kevin Farrell, Kathleen Chalaron, Dennis Farrell, Linda Farrell Townsend, Michael Farrell, and Joe Farrell Jr.

Finally, I'd like to acknowledge and thank the One Presence I call God, who animates all life in the Universe and inspires, guides, protects, and supports each of us during our everlasting physical and non-physical journey through time. My personal connection with God has meant more than anything to me since I was a young child, and it is this Divine Presence who guides me in everything I do.

# ABOUT STEVE FARRELL

In the 1990s, years before Steve Farrell became involved with Humanity's Team, he cofounded and led two high-growth technology companies based in Silicon Valley that were featured in the *INC* 500 list of the fastest growing companies and spanned the United States and Europe. During this period of his life, he was also an officer in the Young Entrepreneurs' Organization and the Young Presidents' Organization.

By all accounts, Steve was living the "good life" at this time, but when he felt a calling to play an active role in creating a consciousness movement that could help people across the globe awaken to their deeper self and the interconnectedness and Oneness of everything in the universe, Steve followed his heart and left the "American Dream" behind. What he found is the story of Humanity's Team and the New Universal Dream.

Steve is the cofounder of Humanity's Team along with Neale Donald Walsch. Both are members of the Evolutionary Leaders Circle. Steve contributed a chapter to the Gold Nautilus, COVR and Living Now Award-winning Evolutionary Leaders' book *Our Moment of Choice: Evolutionary Visions and Hope for the Future*. He lives in Boulder, Colorado, with his wife Stephanie, their two young adults, and their dog Sadie.

*www.humanitysteam.org* and *www.stevecfarrell.com*

# MESSAGE FROM THE PUBLISHER

Light on Light Press produces enhanced content books spotlighting the sacred ground upon which all religious and wisdom traditions intersect. It aims to stimulate and perpetuate engaged interspiritual and perennial wisdom dialogue for the purpose of assisting the dawning of a unitive consciousness that will inspire compassionate action toward a just and peaceful world.

We are delighted to publish *A New Universal Dream* because it illustrates so beautifully how one person's life can do so much to uplift us all. Steve Farrell's life story exemplifies what each of us can do to ensure not only that our own life is on the right track, but also that it contributes to keeping humanity on track, too. This book does so by making it very clear that the experiences described herein reflect our own, by assuring us that we are not limited by wherever we find ourselves, and by reminding us that everything that comes our way is an opportunity for positive change, both for ourselves and others. This is an inspiring story that can serve as guidance for many in how to utilize our expanding consciousness for the betterment of the world. In a time that calls for a light in the darkness, this book provides a beacon in awakening us to the activism the world most needs.

We consider this to be a prototypical autobiography for our time, focusing not only on personal transformation, but also on collective transformation. It is a roadmap for making a difference in the world, an inspiration for making bold, caring, and clear choices in our lives, and a guidebook for changing the future of humanity. It offers many lessons learned in choosing a path in life that benefits the good of the whole. This book shows the way to a new universal dream calling to all of us.


Managing Editors—


Kurt Johnson Ph.D.
Robert Atkinson Ph.D.
Nomi Naeem, M.A.
Chamatkara (Sandra Simon)